FAST CARS and frybread

FAST CARS and frybread

REPORTS FROM THE REZ

by GORDON JOHNSON

Heyday Books, Berkeley, California

BayTree Books

For my children, Tyra, Missy, Brandon, Jared

This book was made possible in part by generous grants from the BayTree Fund and the National Endowment for the Arts.

The *Riverside Press-Enterprise*, in which all columns first appeared, is gratefully acknowledged.

Library of Congress Cataloging-in-Publication Data

Johnson, Gordon.
  Fast cars and frybread : reports from the Rez / Gordon Johnson.
    p. cm.
  ISBN 978-1-59714-066-9 (pbk. : alk. paper)
  1. Indians of North America--California--Pala Indian Reservation--Social life and customs. I. Title.
  E78.C15J57 2007
  305.8009794'98--dc22
                    2007009807

Cover Photograph and Design: Lorraine Rath, with thanks to Jackie Perez-Gratz for permission to photograph "Blue Velvet"
Interior Design/Typesetting: Lorraine Rath
Printing and Binding: McNaughton & Gunn, Saline, MI

Orders, inquiries, and correspondence should be addressed to:
        Heyday Books
        P. O. Box 9145, Berkeley, CA 94709
        (510) 549-3564, Fax (510) 549-1889
        www.heydaybooks.com

Printed in the United States of America on 50% consumer waste recycled paper. ♻

10 9 8 7 6 5 4 3 2 1

Contents

Introduction

There was a time when time wasn't so insistent. It moved slower, held less sway. That was Indian time. These days it's headlong rush, all hurry, hurry, hurry—no time to waste. But as a writer I sought to hold time in place. My impulse as a columnist was to capture the moment, and hold it still.

From 1993 to 2000, I was a newspaper columnist for the *Press-Enterprise* in Riverside County, California, and this book collects forty-three columns written and published during those years. I'm a fifty-five-year-old Cahuilla/Cupeño member of the Pala Indian Reservation, and what follows are life moments I wanted to rescue from change.

Since the advent of casinos, Indians have been window-seat passengers on the streamliner of change. Reservation life has been changing at dizzying speeds. It won't be long before the reservation has little resemblance to what it once was. I want my children and grandchildren to see what rez life was like before cable TV and cell phones and laptop computers. When rez life was closer to the bone, the Redbone. So this book is an act of sharing some of those rez times.

To answer a question I'm frequently asked, I didn't grow up here. My father, a white man, moved us to the Bay Area while he attended Santa Clara University, then Stanford University for his master's degree, then worked for IBM. So I wasn't reared here, but I did live here a couple of years, with my mother and her parents, as a young boy, while my father recovered from tuberculosis in a military hospital. Most of my summers and Christmas vacations were also spent here. Those were impressionable times for me, and the memories run deep.

I moved here permanently after college in 1973 and haven't left. I married a Pala Indian woman and fathered four children. Now many of my children have children, and my grandchildren are from here. And too, the blood and bones of my relatives are here.

So where is here? Pala is a twelve-thousand-acre Indian reservation of about one thousand members in north San Diego County established for the Cupa Indians from the Warner Springs area, and the Luiseño Indians, who traditionally lived here. The Cupeños were evicted from their traditional homelands by a legal system the Indians didn't fathom and removed by force in 1903 to the Pala Reservation—our Trail of Tears. At the reservation's center is Mission San Antonio de Pala, an asistencia of Mission San Luis Rey, built with Indian labor in 1816.

Pala is situated below Palomar Mountain in a semi-arid valley of sage and chamise, about twenty-five miles from the Pacific. The San Luis Rey River, which empties into the Pacific, dissects the reservation and is part of its lifeblood. At one time, the river ran year-round and Indian women visited its banks to launder clothes with washboards and soaproot. Today, however, an upstream dam holds back the water, and the river only flows after heavy rainfall.

Pala Reservation is one of the few patterned after a traditional village, with homes placed on lots close to each other, not far-flung like other reservations. Original Pala homes were thin-walled, two-room prefabs that arrived by ship in 1903, and were assembled without insulation or electricity or indoor toilets. The reservation's unique layout had many outhouses facing an interior road that people affectionately called Toilet Street. I think the closeness of the homes drew Pala people closer. The proximity of neighbors made it easier to visit, easier to share a bottle of bootleg wine, easier to tell a story over the backyard fence.

Storytelling, of course, is the connective tissue of reservation life. Storytelling falls into two major categories. The first involves the myths and legends of the people that go far, far back to the time when there were no people, only beings that were precursors to human beings. The second category recounts the lives and events of people. Let it be known that there is a thin line in the second category between story and gossip. My grandmother was a celebrated storyteller of the second kind. She held court at the kitchen table, with a cup of coffee or a can of Lucky Lager in hand, and treated us not only to cast-iron-fried meals, but tasty stories. When I was a child, we had no TV, no radio, and few books. But we did have my grandmother. It was she, I believe, who instilled in me the appreciation of a good story.

Her stories resonated with me, and maybe cursed me, with the need to be a writer. My whole life, I've earned my living writing, first with a typewriter, then computer. I became a newspaperman so I could write yet earn a steady paycheck to put bacon on the table and buy diapers for my brood. I still write, hoping to give voice to a people that went unheard from for too long.

Before newspapering, I went the University of California, Santa Cruz, as a philosophy major. Philosophy kick-started thoughts of death (it's been said a philosopher lives with one foot in the grave), and I've spent my life trying to make some sense of this existence. I make no claims to progress. To this day, I'm only certain of my uncertainty. But philosophy did activate my curiosity, and prompted me to seek. I sought out stories that helped illuminate life for me. And that led to my career as a columnist, where I had the freedom to explore aspects of humanity and character that might shed light. As an Indian, I also saw a way of life disappearing. I wanted to capture what I could, and put it down on paper so others, years from now, could know a little of Pala. To accomplish this, I made a point of talking to the elders, learning what I could of Indian life that unfolded before my time.

At fifty-five, I'm old enough to have experienced some of Old Pala. From the old-timers I learned about the slower Indian life, before velocity replaced meaning. From contemporaries, I learned how Indian people are accommodating change. We are not museum pieces stuck on a shelf. We continue to evolve. It's up to us to combine the past with the present to make for a better future.

Gordon Johnson
Pala Indian Reservation
October 15, 2006

More Than a Shot in the Dark

September 28, 1993

Saturday before last, I knelt across the peon fire from Tony Pinto, a crafty player in his mid-seventies from the Cuyapaipe Indian Reservation down near the Mexican border.

To the rhythm of the peon songs, I bounced from side to side, grunting with each move, doing my best to ward off the shot I knew Tony would soon make.

Through the smoke and the dancing firelight, I could see Tony sizing me up, his eyes full of mischief beneath the bill of his yellow baseball cap.

Before long, he clapped his hands and pointed to the east.

"Coime!" he shouted, "Tirado con uno."

He got me...

It was fiesta night on the Pala Indian Reservation, and from the nearby ramadas came the familiar smells of frybread sizzling in hot lard and pinto beans simmering in big pots. Kids in white T-shirts stained red with snow-cone juice laughed and kicked up dust while playing "you punched me so I'll punch you." And Indian people from all over roamed the grounds, shaking hands with old acquaintances, drinking beer with new ones.

It was fiesta.

For as long as anyone can remember, fiestas have been part

of the Indian social life, a time for Indians to celebrate being Indian. For many, fiesta is a Bacchanalian revelry of too much food and too much drink. Of sweaty dancing to the electric twang of "Johnny Be Good." Of sidelong glances at the opposite sex from different reservations.

A big part of fiesta, though, is peon. A fiesta without peon is a birthday party without cake.

Peon, for those who have never seen it, is an ancient gambling game played by Indians of Southern California and westernmost Arizona.

With a well-stoked fire as the game's centerpiece, four-man teams square off on either side of the flames. In what is principally a guessing game, each team member is given a set of small bones cut from coyote legs or deer ribs—one painted white and the other black. The opposing team must guess which hand holds the white bone and which holds the black.

Fifteen counting sticks are used to track the number of times the team hiding the bones avoids getting caught. Once all four players on one team are caught, the bones are passed over to the other side and it's their turn to hide.

A *coime*, or referee, officiates the game, and backers stand behind their teams to sing the peon songs as the men (and sometimes women) hide their bones.

Shots, or guesses, are called out by the opposing team. The shots are actually set patterns, so one shot could mean you think all the white bones are to the right. Once shot, players show their hands. Catch all four and you're hot. Miss all four and you feel like crawling under a rock.

On this night, I played with John Chutnicut at one end, King Freeman next to him, and Al Garcia to the right of him. I was kneeling next to Al at the other end.

We had caught three of Tony's teammates, leaving only him still hiding. He sang a peon song so old nobody knew it. So he sang alone. He smiled as he sang, and the light glinted off his silver belt buckle adorned with a turquoise rock bigger than an eagle's calling card.

"Shoot me, shoot me," he taunted.

"Coime, twenty dollars I get him," I said. I reached for a twenty-spot in my pocket and handed it to the coime. Someone on the other side matched my bet.

I studied Tony and decided on the shot.

"Coime, tirado con dos," I said with two fingers pointing to the west.

The grin of victory spread on Tony's face and he sang louder. My hopes went south, and I knew I had missed. There went my money.

We ended up losing that night. And Tony went on to play Leroy Salgado's team from Pechanga for the championship. Pechanga beat Tony and took home the pot, more than six hundred dollars. But Tony opened his wallet and bet three hundred for another game.

The Salgados and Tony's team played again. This time Tony collected the money.

Next time, Tony. See ya in Yuma.

Lighting the Way for the
Dearly Departed

At one end of the living room of my grandmother Delfreda Magee's adobe home, there's an old mahogany hutch where all the plaster statues of the saints stand in proper order. Jesus, Mary, and Joseph in the center, St. Anthony and St. Theresa on either side of them, and so on.

Shortly before dusk today, just as she has for as long as I can remember, she'll slide open the hutch drawer and pull out packages of store-bought candles.

As is her habit, she'll arrange the candles in a grocery bag—paper, not plastic—in careful rows so as not to break them.

When she feels they're safe, she'll roll the top of the bag down into a good handle, and set it on the table.

Then she'll sit on the edge of her chair, and wait.

It won't be a patient wait. It'll be the kind of wait where she'd check her watch every minute if she had one. One of those "If someone doesn't pick me up soon, it'll mean nobody cares about me" kinds of waits.

Usually a son or daughter or grandchild or some other relative will feel her vibes from a couple of blocks away and come get her.

But if a ride is too long in coming, she'll grab the bag and head out the door, closing it a little harder than necessary.

In a huff, she'll light out in a half-trot for the graveyard, taking faster steps than any eighty-year-old woman has a right to.

"Don't they care?" she'll mumble in a pout. "This is All Souls Day, and I've got to get to candle lighting. People today have no respect."

The Pala Indian Reservation cemetery isn't more than four blocks as the crow flies from her house, but she won't make it a quarter of the way before someone passing will give her a lift.

Cars and pickup trucks will stir up the dust as they pull into the dirt parking area in front of the graveyard.

Once she passes through the cemetery gate, she'll feel better. In the gathering darkness she'll take the familiar path to my grandfather Paul Magee's grave.

My grandfather's headstone is cut from the black granite of the quarry his father once worked. At the headstone's center, there's a picture of him that I took at one of my kids' birthday parties several years before he died.

It's a favorite likeness of him, when he still had the fun-loving eyes and the good-times smile. Not the deadpan gaze that came after the stroke.

Anyway, when she gets to his grave near the back of the cemetery, she'll begin the work of lighting the candles, letting a little melted wax drip onto a spot and then setting the candle into it so it won't tip over.

She'll light dozens of candles, enough to go around the whole concrete slab of his grave and over the top of his headstone, all the while praying for his soul.

Intermingled with the prayers, she'll talk to him, reliving the better times, filling him in on the latest news about his children and grandchildren, gently scolding him for leaving without her.

When the candles are lighted, she'll stand back for a moment, drawing her knitted white sweater a little closer to her body to ward off the chill of loneliness.

By this time, the graveyard will be crowded with people who have come to light candles for their dead. And she'll stop and talk in low tones to friends and relatives, exchanging stories about the departed.

And she'll make the rounds to the graves of her brothers and sisters and mother and father and all the other loved ones who have preceded her to the other side, stopping to light candles at each one.

Soon the Pala Mission padre will arrive to bless the graves, walking along the freshly raked pathways, sprinkling holy water as he goes.

Before leaving, she'll stop one more time at my grandfather's grave. And she'll stand in the soft glow of a thousand burning candles, full of the memories of all those she's cared about, full of the pang of missing them.

It's then that I want to walk up to her, put my arm around her shoulders, give her a squeeze of assurance, and say, "I love you, Grandmother."

Homespun Tales from the Front Porch

JANUARY 18, 1994

By the time I got to his porch Sunday afternoon, my buddy Jean Jackson was halfway done skinning a coyote he'd trapped earlier that morning, and Robert K. Thompson and Hank Howard were a couple of beers each into a twelve-pack.

For more than thirty years now, Jackson's front porch on the Pala Indian Reservation has been a magnet for people from the fringe, the people who like pickled eggs and home-cured olives with their beer, the people who don't mind a little English mixed in with their cuss words.

The porch extends out from a cabin that Jackson built over the years with scrap lumber salvaged from a lifetime of construction jobs. From the walls and ceiling hang an array of deer antlers, dried rattlesnake skins, old snowshoes, mystery rocks, and flycatchers.

And if you wipe away the dust and the cobwebs, you can read the porch's motto tacked to the wall: "We don't have a town drunk, we all take turns."

Now, I don't want to give the wrong impression. Not everyone who takes a seat on Jackson's porch drinks. But damn few don't.

Over the last quarter of a century of hanging out at his porch, I have toasted the health of so many others that I've almost ruined my own. On this day, however, I teetotaled. Not as much fun, but I'm bound and determined to lose this beer belly.

Whether I'm imbibing or not, I like Jean's porch. You get to meet a lot of people, and hear a lot of stories, some of which are actually true.

On this warm afternoon, I talked to Hammerin' Hank Howard, one of Temecula Valley's more colorful old-timers.

Despite eighty-three years of work-filled days and wine-filled nights, Hank Howard possesses a world-class memory. Even when he's tuned up, he can tell you on what day in 1927 he bought a pair of shoes and how much they cost.

And speaking of shoes, he wears size thirteens. And his work-thickened hands are huge. In Temecula Valley, Hammerin' Hank Howard is a legend.

He reads without glasses, eats without teeth, and lives without worries.

Except for an Army stint during the Big One, Hank has spent his entire life in the area.

Born July 19, 1909, on the Howard Ranch, as a kid he harvested barley with mowers drawn by teams of twenty or more horses on the same land where Rainbow Canyon homeowners on Via Eduardo now manicure their lawns with the latest in mulching mowers.

Hank's dad, Grant Ulysses Howard, came to Temecula in 1894 from Wisconsin. His mother, Katherine, was a Ludy whose father, Jake, had immigrated here from Germany in the 1850s.

Grant and Katherine married in 1899 and set up household. The Howard family—there were seven children, but three took sick and died young—lived in a fourteen-room, two-story ranch house overlooking Wolf Valley. Times were tough when Hank was a kid, especially when crop prices hit bottom. There were days when young Hank had to lace up his clodhoppers with baling wire because he didn't have money for store-bought shoestrings.

At least he didn't have far to walk to school. The old schoolhouse was on his dad's land near Wolf's tomb. Hank and school didn't mix well, and he never got past the eighth grade.

When Hank was eleven, his mother took off with another man, so Hank had to work even harder to make up for her absence.

To help put food on the table, Hank hunted and trapped. In his lifetime, he's killed more than one hundred and forty deer, many on the back side of Palomar Mountain. But his favorite Springfield .30-06 rifle was stolen several years ago by some hippies, he said. "I'd still like to get that gun back."

In 1922, when wheat prices went to eighty cents per hundred pounds, the Howards had a bumper crop on the 750 acres they farmed. His father bought 412 acres on Pala Road in north San Diego County for four thousand dollars. The land was originally homesteaded by John Welty, owner of the Welty Hotel in Old Town Temecula.

Most of the property was sold over the years, but Hank lives on what's left.

Hank's been married four times and is currently eligible.

"You got any kids, Hank?" I asked.

"Not yet," he replied, finishing off another can of beer.

A Hawk's Cry, a Dusty Saddle, and Memories

APRIL 12, 1994

Here, tucked away in the mountains of the Santa Ysabel Indian Reservation, where wild turkeys still roam, the urban madness was an eternity away.

We were standing on the rocky ledge of a waterfall, watching a graceful stream wriggle its way around water-smoothed boulders to plummet one hundred and fifty feet straight down into a green pool below.

A gray and rainy mist clung to hilltops lush with spring grass and oak trees, and mean-looking clouds rolled above the landscape all the way to the ocean and beyond.

"Ain't this place something? I told you it was great," said my buddy Jimmy Balcone. "I grew up here, this is where I played as a kid."

A hawk cried out in the canyon, and water rumbled against the rocks. And that was it. Sacred silence.

Earlier that afternoon, Balcone and I had been sitting around shooting the breeze at Jean Jackson's house in Pala when Balcone said, "Hey, Jean, why don't you show Gordon the arrowhead I found."

Jean opened his wallet, pulled out an arrowhead and handed it to me.

I laid it in the palm of my hand and marveled at it. Less than a nickel's width across and thin as a stick of gum. Some Indian guy a hundred or more years ago spent hours chipping flakes off a piece of chert and, with skill and patience, ended up with this bit of perfection.

"A guy in town offered me fifty dollars for it, but I wouldn't sell it. I gave it to Jean as a friend," Balcone said.

"Where did you find it?" I asked.

"By the waterfall, below my house," he said. "Someday we can go there."

"How about now?"

"How about it?"

We jumped into my old war pony, the world's ugliest Datsun diesel pickup, and drove east up Highway 76 to Lake Henshaw, then turned south toward the reservation.

"First you have to meet my aunt, she's a kick," Balcone said.

His seventy-six-year-old aunt, Rena Sotelo, lives alone in a single-wide, twenty-five-foot trailer manufactured in the 1950s. About ten years ago, her boys added a room just big enough for a wood cookstove.

No electricity, no refrigeration, no TV, not even a dog.

"You don't like dogs?" I asked.

"Naw, they crap all over my flowers," she said, in the clipped diction of Indians who know their language.

She wore a knit skullcap, a long sweater, a flower-print blouse, green slacks, and tennis shoes, and she had fiery eyes that could see into people.

Her only contact with the outside world was a battery-operated transistor radio next to the kerosene lantern on the small kitchen table. All day, she listened to news and to talk shows, and she knew more about world events than I did.

One thing for sure, she didn't like bureaucrats calling Indians "minorities." "This is our land, these are our homes.

Why should they call us 'minorities' in our own homes?" she questioned.

After we left her, and we were bouncing down the dirt road toward the falls, I said to Balcone, "That's one heck of a lady."

"She's been a mother to me," he said, nodding.

On the way back from the falls, we stopped at Balcone's home, a two-room adobe built by his grandfather in 1903.

The old ranch saddle still sat on the rack beneath the front porch, but the horses and cattle were long gone. Balcone prefers beer to beef.

We went inside and started a fire in the big fireplace his grandfather made with sweat and mortar and rocks from down below.

"I never knew my father, and my mother dumped me off here when I was a baby," he said. "So I was raised here by my grandparents and with my aunt up the road."

He told me how, when he was fourteen, his grandfather died in the bed over near the window. "Just let me go, boy, just say goodbye," were his grandfather's last words, as Balcone gave him a final hug.

Shortly after returning from Vietnam, Balcone found his grandmother lying outside, barely breathing from a heart attack, and he tried to revive her with the techniques he'd used on men sucking wind through chest wounds in the rice paddies.

But she too died.

And there, by the yellow glow of the fire, with the rain thumping on the roof, I saw a tear glisten in the corner of his eye.

That was when the old adobe seemed to shudder, then sigh.

When Walking Doesn't Cure
What Ails You

JUNE 21, 1994

The June sun has baked the green out of the hillside grasses. When I step off the trail, the grass crackles underfoot, and bleached foxtails cling to my pant legs.

It's the red-ant time, when thousands march in single file from the anthill to the fallen dead sparrow, only to march back again, clutching decayed flesh in fiery jaws.

It's the hot time, when the white sun burns a hole in the pale sky.

Yes, it's danged hot, with gnats flitting about my head, and powdery dust flying with each footfall.

But I keep to the trail, sweat-soaked T-shirt sticking to my back, throat longing for an ice-cold Pepsi. I walk, wandering through wilting white sage and scrub brush.

I'm just walking, no place in mind, just need to be moving.

Sometimes, when the blues take me down, when self-pity swallows me up, and life seems like one big hangover, walking helps.

I don't know why I get like this. Everything is going okay, I guess. No major problems. But every now and then I get this hollow ache inside, and the world gets bleak, and I feel like hell.

When I get this way, there's no escaping it. Might as well roll with the punches, I say.

I keep walking.

There, half buried in the sand, I see an old coffee can, rusted so badly I can't tell if the MJB is really there or if it's just a heat trick.

I remember I used to drink coffee from a thick mug at Julia McCormick's house on the Rincon Reservation.

We'd sit around her kitchen table and practice Indian songs before going out to sweat with her husband, Therman, in the lodge at the side of the house.

It was a great house—branding irons, cast-iron kettles, and wire cutters hanging under the front porch that overlooks the pasture where years ago cattle were penned, earmarked, and branded.

Therman was our teacher, a man who did his best to see that old ways would live. But he died a while back, leaving Julia to carry on as best she could.

Julia was die-hard Indian. White-haired and frail, but doctor's warnings be damned, she'd come to the peon games anyway, ready to sing. I can still see her propped in a lawn chair, wrapped in a sleeping bag, with the reds and yellows and blues of the fire reflected in her glasses.

"Come on, boys, let's win," she'd say.

Last week, her singing days ended, however, after her eighty-one-year-old heart finally gave out. And Saturday, we shoveled dirt into her grave on the La Jolla Indian Reservation.

Adios, Julia. And thanks.

I keep walking.

Across the river, I turn left by the cactus patch where I once shot cottontails as a kid. Can't shoot there anymore, though; too many houses nearby. But I go down a ways to where the wind and rain have sculpted a steep bank of red earth until it looks as wrinkled and rutted as an old man's face.

I'm reminded of old Uncle Jack. He and the other viejos used to hide out down here sometimes to drink wine in peace, far from the scowls of women.

He had a thicket of silvery hair, and dark leathery skin carved by time. Mostly he wore khaki pants, white T-shirts, and work boots, the kind we kids called clodhoppers. I'm not sure where he came from, but I've been told he was from Old Pala, a Luiseño Indian who was at Pala before the Cupeño Indians were forced out of Warner Springs and relocated here in 1903.

To me, he was scary. He looked at you with dark eyes, burning with some inner power. When relatives of sick people would come to him for help, he'd go to his shadowy bedroom in my Aunt Martha's house, reach under his pillow, and pull out his medicine pouch. I don't know what was in there, I doubt if anybody does. But whatever it was, it worked. More than one person walked the earth longer by way of Uncle Jack's power.

They say, however, every cure steals a bit of your own life force. It was my cousin who found Uncle Jack the day his power ran out. He died thirty years ago in the outhouse, all used up.

I keep walking.

Don't think so much about death, I say. Kind of hard not to, I say.

I keep walking.

Nothing Like a Sweat to Cure
What Ails You

SEPTEMBER 20, 1994

Yellow and orange flames leap skyward from the sweat fire like dancing church spires.

At its heart, the fire burns blue and white, and football-size lava rocks sandwiched between the flaming oak logs glow red.

The fire's soft light envelops the sweat lodge on the banks of the San Luis Rey River as it cuts through the Pala Indian Reservation.

Several big oak trees stand sentry to the dome-shaped lodge. Through gaps in the overhanging branches, you can see the stars shine like glitter on black velvet.

On the tin windbreak surrounding the fire, you can see the shadow of Mark Mojado, who tends the fire with a pitchfork, making sure the rocks heat evenly.

Sitting on a nearby bench, John Chutnicut hand-rolls a cigarette with tobacco from a Prince Albert can.

Also on the bench, King Freeman pets a couple of his son's Rottweilers that like to hang around the lodge, and Richard "Onnie" Mojado chews sunflower seeds.

Over by the faucet, Randall "Doc" Majel fills a small pot with water and sage leaves for tea that will brew on hot coals.

The talk is easy and familiar. These guys have known each other most of their lives.

With the fire going good and the tea brewing, Mark asks, "Well, men, should we sing a few?"

"May as well, can't dance," someone else replies.

The men find seats, clear their throats, and the songs begin. Haunting chants so old that the meanings of many words have blurred with time.

"Ha-na-na-way-oh-na, ha-na-na-way-oh-na, ha-na-na-way-oh-na, meno-ken-ah," the song goes, voices flowing in unison.

When the song ends, coyotes yip in the distance.

"They want to sing, too," Johnny says, and he starts the coyote song.

"Ya-he, trama-way-oh-na, ya-he, trama-way-oh-na, oy-ya-koy-ya-way-oh-na…"

With the rocks to the point where they aren't gonna get any hotter, the men disrobe to enter the lodge.

Mark, who has recently returned from Sun Dancing in Utah, leads the sweat and is first to crawl in. The others follow, forming a circle around the pit at the lodge's center.

Rocks are carried into the lodge with the pitchfork, and Mark uses deer antlers to position the rocks in the pit.

The entrance flaps drop, and the lodge goes black, save for the lava rocks, which glow like feral eyes in a darkened cave.

Mark starts the prayers, first to The Grandfather, then to the four directions, then to the world of spirits.

He sprinkles a mixture of tobacco and sweet grass on the hot rocks and it lights up like sparklers on the Fourth of July, filling the lodge with aromatic smoke.

Starting to the leader's left, each man in turn prays aloud. It is forbidden to repeat these prayers outside the lodge.

But for Indian people, the sweat lodge is a descent into the womb of Mother Earth to reunite with the spiritual world we hold sacred. It is a purification ritual, a purging of wrongdoings, a way to restore balance in our lives.

During the prayers, Mark ladles out water from a bucket onto the rocks and steam billows into the lodge with a gentle hiss.

Sweat seeps from the body in rivulets, and you can feel it trail down your skin, taking with it all that is putrid, leaving behind only what is pure.

More songs follow the prayers, and the flaps are lifted so the steam can rush out and carry the prayers and songs to the heavens.

Three times this is done, with fresh rocks brought in for each round. The fourth round is for strength, and the heat bears down on you, until you wonder if you can take it anymore. But you dig deep and hold on, because you sense that the suffering you do here may help those in need: the sick, the elderly, the people lost on the dark road.

After the sweat is done, and everyone has showered and toweled dry, Onnie shovels coals from the fire into a barbecue and grills hamburgers made from ground elk meat.

It is time to relax around the fire, eating and joking, and for now anyway, all is right with the world.

As Spirits of the Old Ones Dance, We Sing

MAY 2, 1995

A gossamer mist, soft and wispy, billowed from the branches of scrub oak and tamarisk as spirits of the night breezed by.

And the night sky, made starless by drifting clouds, seemed somehow expectant, waiting for some kind of deliverance.

On this night, thirty of us gathered in a small clearing at the foot of Hot Springs Mountain and stared out at the shadowy landscape, looking at nothing in particular, mostly listening to dead calm.

Then gourd rattles broke the silence, shaking out syncopated rhythms; and voices led by Leroy Miranda Jr. sang Cupeño bird songs, songs not heard by these mountains for some one hundred years.

We had come back to Cupa, our ancestral village at Warner Springs in north San Diego County, for a night of song and sweat to pay homage to the old ones who preceded us in death here.

Once, this had been our land, where we birthed our children, prayed to our Creator, suffered our injuries, celebrated our triumphs, and died our quiet deaths.

The hot springs here had been our power, the wild game and plants our sustenance. Our lives and this land were one.

But in 1902, we lost our land in federal courts. Seems we didn't have proper title, even though we had been on this land for as long as anyone could remember.

Governor John Gately Downey, who took over this land from John Trumbull Warner, who got it from the Mexicans, who got it from the Spanish, who grabbed it from the Cupeños, had plans for the land. His plans didn't include a bunch of red-skinned squatters messing up the place.

So in May 1903, armed soldiers encircled the thatch-roofed adobe homes and ordered people to pack what they could into mule-drawn wagons and leave. Simple as that.

Women wailed, babies cried, men resisted as best they could, but eventually most complied, except for the disconsolate few who, in fist-shaking rage, fled into the mountains, never to be heard from again.

It was a forty-mile trek from Cupa down to their new home on the Pala Indian Reservation. To this day, Cupeños refer to it as the Trail of Tears.

And so we came to Cupa on this night to honor our dead.

Cans of Prince Albert tobacco, painted gourd rattles, bamboo clackers, and a small hide-covered drum rested gently on the dirt mound at the sweat lodge's entrance. A short staff topped with an outstretched eagle's talon and two eagle feathers wrapped with red yarn stood guard over it all.

We smudged our bodies with smoke from dried sage, and one by one filed into the sweat lodge, the womb of Mother Earth.

Hot rocks, glowing red from the fire, were placed at the lodge's center, and the canvas flap was lowered.

The sweat leader, Tubby Lavato, poured water carried from the nearby hot springs onto the rocks. The rocks hissed, and the steam smelled of sulfur.

First came the prayers, offerings from the heart. Then came more songs, voices raised in reverence to the old ways and the old ones.

After an hour or so, the rocks were spent. So another batch was brought in, and the ceremony continued.

The heat was stifling, legs cramped, backs ached from leaning forward. But it was good to suffer for the people.

Sweat flowed in rivulets from the body, spilling into the sand to mingle with the blood, sweat, and tears of our forebears.

When it was all over, we toweled off by the fire.

"It has always been a dream of mine to have a sweat up here," Miranda said. "It sure felt good."

"I know what you mean," said Lavato. "I could see them, the women in long dresses, the men in white shirts and Levis, dancing and laughing. I think we made them happy," Lavato said.

Plates piled high with a meat-and-potato stew and frybread were passed around. And the talk was quiet and the laughter gentle as we feasted.

From where we sat, we could see the cemetery below, where wooden crosses marked the graves of long-dead Cupeños.

Rest easy, my people, you have not been abandoned.

Nights of Fast Cars, Fisticuffs, and Fiesta Fun

JULY 18, 1995

Everything seemed wide open back then. Pure wildness.

You could smell it in the dust kicked up by the muscled-up cars with racing slicks and rapping pipes as they spun into the dirt parking lot. You could hear it in the untamed laughter erupting from the revelers gathered around the pickups weighted down with ice chests filled with beer. You could see it in the don't-mess-with-me sneers flashed by the buffalo-shouldered bad boys at the outsiders who ventured in.

These were the classic fiesta nights on the Rincon Indian Reservation in north San Diego County in the early 1970s. They just don't make 'em like that anymore.

At the center of it all was the old tribal hall, a worn-out building painted a kind of lime green. The glass windows, long ago busted out, had been replaced with sheets of heavy wire mesh. The wooden floor was polished smooth by countless years of leather soles jitterbugging, slow dancing, and doing the Rincon Stomp.

To the rear was the bar where Ed Arviso or Berkeley Calac or some other barkeep would fish icy longnecks out of the ice chest and hand them across the counter to you for seventy-five cents.

Up front was the small bandstand where Fat Boy Banegas and Frankie Orosco and the Chaipos brothers, Harold and Beaver, would set up their amps and microphones and tune up.

At nine o'clock or so, the music started. Fat Boy would fire up Van Morrison's "Domino" and the folks would file in. Pay two dollars at the door and get your hand stamped. Those who couldn't afford the admission clustered at the windows to at least hear the music and check out the dancers.

Mostly the guys wore white T-shirts, blue jeans, and cowboy boots. Ballplayers who played in the softball tournament before the dance never bothered to change; they danced in their uniforms—Pauma Men's Club, Pala, Rincon, Soboba, Morongo, Barona, and more.

The girls gussied up some, painting their eyes with a multi-hued feline sweep, teasing their hair to give it loft, squeezing their rumps into the white hotpants popular at the time.

By eleven, the dance sizzled. Fat Boy would be bopping with Sam and Dave's "Knock on Wood" and the old house jumped. The guys danced tough. The girls wriggled plenty.

Once or twice a night, someone would yell "fight" and everyone would vacate the dance floor to see who was scrapping outside. In those days, it was mostly one on one. Two guys squared off, fists flying, and you could hear the smack of knuckles against flesh when someone landed one. Eventually they'd clinch and hit the ground, wrestling in the dirt, throwing punches when they could.

The fight would go until somebody got knocked out or was too hurt to fight back. Then the onlookers would jump in and break it up.

An hour later, you'd see the two combatants, fat-lipped and swollen-jawed, drinking beer with each other, laughing and joking like nothing had happened.

That's the way it was back then. More like sport than anything serious. Now it's guns and knives.

The ramadas, willow-covered frames where people set up

makeshift kitchens to sell food, formed an L around the dance hall.

Whole families helped with the cooking chores. Women rolled out tortilla dough and cut bacon for the beans. Men fried hamburger and diced chilies for the salsa. Kids served sodas and coffee.

Most had tables out front for customers to sit and eat. Nothing like sitting down to a big plate of steaming tacos, piled high with hot salsa, grease dribbling down your chin.

And Leroy Salgado's family had a great steak burrito, and you couldn't go wrong at Lucille Lugo's ramada for tamales and beans.

Behind the dance hall, the peon fires burned. Some of the old-timers were still alive back then and you'd see guys like Sam Brown and Raphael Tortes, guys so old they could look straight into your soul, grunting, singing, and calling out shots.

The dance would usually end at two a.m., but only the older folks would go home. The young would stay and howl at the moon till dawn. Then greet the sun with a bowl of menudo and a last beer.

Finally, home to saw a few logs and wake up in time to do it all over again the next night.

Somethin' else, those Rincon fiesta nights.

Boy and Dog Take a Walk
to the Store

Me and Frosty, the Airedale mix that strayed into our yard and never left, were playing tug of war with a knotted sock when my grandmother yelled from the front porch.

"Gooorrrdddooonnn," she screeched in a pitch so high that Tommy Portillo's hogs down the way squealed with thoughts of getting slopped.

"Yeah, Gram," I said, peeking my head around the corner of the adobe house.

"Oh, there you are. I need you to run up to the store for me. Here's a quarter, get a dozen corn tortillas so I can finish these enchiladas," she said.

"Okay," I replied. "But can I get candy if there's change left?"

"I guess. But hurry, boy. I gotta get dinner on. Remember, now, corn tortillas, not flour."

"Corn tortillas," I repeated.

I shoved the quarter deep into my jeans' pocket. I was only five, and hadn't handled much silver in my life. With a sense of importance, I headed up the road. Frosty, his stub of a tail wagging, led the way.

It was early fall, but the afternoon sun still had zing enough to make the asphalt of Pala Mission Road feel tacky on the bottoms of my bare feet. I hurried to cross it.

Towering eucalyptus trees shaded the powdery dirt on the other side and I sifted my toes through it to cool them off.

While there, I spied a couple of Lucky Lager cans, tall ones, glinting from beneath some gourd leaves near a rusted wire fence. Tall cans made the best horseshoes.

I grabbed the cans, found a good-sized rock, and plopped down into the dirt to work on them. Within minutes, I had the cans pounded out and formed to my feet. Sure, they pinched a little on the sides, but not bad.

With high steps, I clip-clopped down the tarmac, pretending I was Doughboy, my uncle Jimmy Banks's white horse, the one he rode each year at the front of the Corpus Christi procession.

Like Doughboy, I trotted sideways, throwing my head back to whinny and snort. I did that past Fernando Ortega's house, and past Bill Shoulder's, but before I got to Aunt Kitty's place on the corner, I stopped and pulled the cans off my feet. Aunt Kitty had a big yellow-eyed dog—part hound and part hellion—that slept on her porch.

I was hoping to sneak by unnoticed, but fifteen feet from the house, Frosty's neck hairs bristled, his legs stiffened, and a low, menacing growl rumbled deep in his chest.

The growl, I'm sure, alerted the sleeping dog, and he bounded off the porch, lunging toward us, barking and snarling with fangs bared.

Never one to back off, Frosty leaped at the charging dog and the fight was on. The dogs wrestled for position on their hind legs, both seeking advantage to the neck, but neither able to sink in for a good hold.

Aunt Kitty's dog was probably twenty pounds heavier, but Frosty was faster. The two dogs boiled out into the street, bodies slamming, teeth clashing, Frosty giving as good as he got.

The yellow-eyed dog dropped his head for a lock on Frosty's

front leg, giving Frosty a chance to latch onto the base of the hound's long ear. Frosty ripped at the ear, shaking his head like a javelina in a hornets' nest.

Unable to counterattack, the yellow-eyed dog stopped fighting, which in dog lingo is like saying "uncle." Frosty let go and limped toward me. I looked him over. He had a couple of bite holes in him, but nothing a few licks with his tongue and some time wouldn't heal.

We walked on.

At the corner of the park across from the store, my heart sank. My grandfather sat at the old man's bench, which was just a couple of boards nailed between the trunks of two eucalyptus trees.

On the ground between another old-timer and my grandfather was a half-full bottle of Gallo port.

The sun glistened off my grandfather's greasy alcohol sheen. His right eye drooped, his mouth hung slack. A purple dribble stained his white T-shirt. His button-fly jeans were unbuttoned. He was messed up. The man with him was no better. They slurred at each other, neither knowing what the other was saying.

Oh, man, drunk again. My gut knotted with worry. It's hard when someone you love falters. I felt ashamed for him.

I got the tortillas, and got out of there fast.

Better Not to Ask for Whom
the Bell Tolls

Sunday morning, an off-key male voice croaked amid the lilting females as the churchgoers sang, "Holy, Holy, Holy, Lord God Almighty..."

He didn't seem to notice or care much that his singing blighted the rest. He simply forged ahead in tone-deaf bliss.

Listening to him, I cracked a smile as I climbed the twelve steps of the Mission San Antonio de Pala's campanile just outside the chapel's open windows.

I go up there now and then, just to get reacquainted with the bells. I like to run my fingers along the raised lettering of the Latin inscription, which translates to "Jesus, Redemptor of Mankind (IHR) Holy God, Mighty One, Holy Immortal One. Have mercy on us. Year of our Lord 1816." Heavy stuff for a bell, wouldn't you say?

The brass plaque embedded in the concrete base says the bell tower was built by Padre Antonio Peyri, the Franciscan friar who established the mission as an asistencia to Mission San Luis Rey in 1816.

But I'm sure he had some help from the Luiseño Indians who lived in Pala at the time.

It's funny how something like a bell tower can insinuate itself into your life.

When I was a kid, my uncle Bob Magee carved an image of the bell tower into the flat side of a baseball-sized rock. I painted it, daubing in the pale blue sky and the whitewashed adobe and the greenery in front. My mother still has that rock. She keeps it in a glass display case along with some of our other family memorabilia.

In front of the bell tower there's a fountain made of river rock, where big goldfish circled in the green, brackish water. Tourists dropped coins into the fountain to make wishes come true. On hot summer days the priest made our wishes come true by rounding us up to clean the fountain of algae and trash. Then we'd get to divvy up the change we gathered from the bottom. With our cutoffs still wet, we'd race to the Pala Store across the street for penny candy. It was a big deal for us, because money was hard to come by for a kid in those days.

On weekdays, at 6:30 a.m., the priest would ring the bells to get people up in time for Mass at 7:00. My grandmother always had breakfast cooked by then. We'd breakfast together—Gram, Gramps, and I—and then she'd tie a scarf around her head and dash out the front door for church.

It was the same for her every morning.

Later, after I got married, my wife and I stayed in a small trailer across the street from the mission. Being so close, I got to intimately know the peal of those bells. Especially after a wild Saturday night. Oh, my aching head.

Thumbtacked on the wall next to my computer in the old trailer-now-office where I write is an 11-by-14-inch historical photograph of the bell tower.

Taken circa 1900, by Lord knows who, the photo was snapped in winter, with the trees stripped of leaves and Palomar Mountain capped in snow.

Three Luiseño Indians occupy the foreground. At play in a freshly dug trench is a girl wearing a straw bonnet. Standing next to her is a dark, heavy-set woman in a long dress and white apron, presumably the girl's mother. She's holding a broom. Next to her is a man, probably her mate, in a work shirt, black vest, faded jeans, and a felt hat. He's leaning on a hoe. They're working at something but I've never quite figured out what.

It's an eerie photo. One I never tire of. The Pala countryside looks so untamed, so desolate. Hardly seems like the same place.

Anyway, I prize the old picture.

Over the years, the bells have punctuated my life. They rang at my wedding, at the baptisms of my children, at the funerals of my grandparents.

When someone dies on the reservation, the bells ring out in the traditional death knell. Everyone knows the slow cadence. "Uh-oh, I wonder who died," the people will say. Within minutes the news spreads across backyards until the whole community knows it has been diminished by one.

I touch the old bells, knowing that, someday, they will toll for me.

At Play with the Gods
at High Altitude

November 7, 1995

King Freeman's Chevy pickup pulled up to the house at 7:00 a.m. Late, as usual. He was supposed to be by at 6:30.

"Had to fix a water pipe at the store this morning," he said, as I climbed into the pickup. King owns the Pala Store across from the mission.

"No big deal," I told him. "I figured you'd be running on Indian time anyway."

King and I have been friends for twenty years or more. Somewhere along the line, our bloodlines cross, so we're even distant cousins. He's sixty now, with hair as white as thistledown. But his hair was white thirty years ago, so no one notices it much. I think he was probably frightened by a mirror.

We were on a mission. For years, I've driven by the Morongo Indian Reservation and been tempted by San Jacinto Peak in the distance. I've always wanted to get to its top. So we were on our way to do just that. King had been up there before, so he was the guide.

A few minutes out of the scrublands of Hemet, we were up in Idyllwild, where the pine trees crowd around oh-so-quaint boutiques and even the Bank of America is in a woodsy A-frame.

We got our permits at the ranger station and parked the truck at Humber Park, where Devil's Slide Trail begins.

At the trailhead, I put on my daypack. I had packed a liter of water and a liter of malted Ovaltine, two Steel Bars for energy and protein, three oranges, a knife, an emergency cigarette lighter, and a small flashlight, just in case we didn't make it off the mountain before dark.

"Ready?" King asked.

"Let's get it," I said.

With muscles reluctant, we took off. Immediately the trail climbed. There would be eight miles of ascent. At Humber Park's elevation of 6,280 feet, the air was already thin. It didn't take long to start puffing.

But it was a grand morning. Cool in shade of the evergreens. Warm where the sun splashed into the clearings. Pine needles and altitude scenting the air.

The trail, built by the Civilian Conservation Corps in the early 1930s, rose in gradual switchbacks through great stands of pines, the soil crisscrossed with waffle-soled hiking boots.

I myself bought new hiking boots for the walk. I've always owned the old-style hunting boots, with high tops for ankle support and lug soles for gripping power. They are rugged, but heavy as anvils after a while.

The new boots were featherlight—part nylon, part rough-out suede. Fearful of blisters, I donned two pairs of socks. But I needn't have worried. Nestled in the boots' padding, my feet felt swaddled in baby blankets.

The trail swung by the base of Tahquitz Rock, a mammoth granite outcropping, saw-toothed and ominous. Some local Indians believe it is the home of Tahquitz, a demigod trickster, who descends from the rock in the form of ball lightning or dust devils to sweep up young maidens for his dining pleasure.

Daredevil rock climbers scale the rock's vertical face. You won't find many Indians, however, messing around up there. Why ask for trouble?

Still higher. The landscape truly takes the breath away. We walked through ferns the color of sunbursts. Through manzanitas of muted greens. Through needle-tipped briar patches. Through moonscapes of eroded granite boulders. Water from cienagas trickled in rivulets across the trail. Red-tailed hawks wheeled in the pale blue sky. Crows scolded us from the gnarled branches of giant pines blackened by lightning.

Then we reached a saddle where we could see to the Coachella Valley and the desert mountains beyond.

We kept going. King complained of aching hips and leg cramps. He told me to go on without him. I kicked it into gear, the hours spent on the stair-stepper in the gym paying off.

At the top, I stood on the highest rock, at 10,804 feet, and surveyed the mountains and valleys. I turned my face skyward and closed my eyes. With the wind biting at my cheeks, for one unearthly moment, I felt airborne, at play with the gods in the sky.

Then I ate. Nothing like ice-cold Ovaltine while sitting on top of the world.

Songs Smooth the Way for Final Passage

JANUARY 9, 1996

Atop a small rise on the Cahuilla Indian Reservation, Our Lady of the Snows Catholic Church glowed in the darkness like a luminous dial on a black-faced watch.

To the east, the round moon angled above the Santa Rosa Mountains and stars dusted the lampblack sky.

It was cold enough for the kids outside to blow steam, and white smoke curled from a new galvanized stovepipe on the church's pitched roof.

Inside, a kid fed lengths of pine and manzanita into a potbellied stove to warm the thirty or so people seated in wooden pews.

In front of the altar, Rosalie Lugo Valencia, still wearing her blue glasses, nestled in the white quilts of her pewter-gray casket.

Last week, Rosalie's seventy-nine-year-old heart came to a standstill. And Friday night, the people gathered for her velorio.

In Indian Country, it is customary to hold wakes for those who kept the old ways.

Born in Cahuilla near Anza, Rosalie learned basket making as a girl from her aunt Mary Lugo Segundo, a well-known traditional basketmaker, who taught Rosie how to weave native grasses into works of art.

Along with Donna Largo from the Santa Rosa Indian Reservation, Rosie helped revive Cahuilla basketry, teaching the old techniques to all who asked to learn.

Tonight, in some small way, she was being repaid.

"Beloved Rosie," read the silk banner draped across the white carnations and pink roses bunched on her casket.

Other bouquets, trimmed with baby's breath, crowded about her. Candles burned in tall silver candlesticks. The grave cross, wrapped in black, leaned against the altar. And bolts of printed fabric covered walls and windows to discourage uninvited spirits.

Funeral singers sat in folding chairs facing Rosie, chanting the songs for the dead.

The first group—Robert Levi, Katherine Siva Saubel, Alvino Siva, Raymond Marcus, and Kim Marcus—sang Cahuilla songs.

Katherine led the songs, Alvino shook out the rhythms with a gourd rattle.

For some songs, Kim danced a kind of slow shuffle, folding his arms, exhaling in soft bursts, dancing as it has been done for hundreds of years.

At one point, Katherine stood on uncertain legs to sing, steadying herself on the edge of the casket. As the old songs rolled off her lips, she looked down at Rosie, her old, laughing friend now silenced. Tears welled in her eyes. The song quivered in her throat.

Katherine sat back down and dabbed her eyes with tissue. All remained quiet while she composed herself. In a minute or so, she regained her voice, and the songs continued.

Outside, Luiseño funeral singers Mark Macarro, Randall Majel, and Raymond Basquez sat in a pentagon-shaped windbreak of tin panels, warming themselves at the fire.

Mark, chairman of the Pechanga Indian Reservation and longtime student of Luiseño culture, said there are about three hundred Luiseño funeral songs in existence. His group sings about one hundred and twenty-five of them, and they continue to learn more.

The songs are prayers, telling of creation and recounting the exploits of deities who were the precursors to man.

The songs help lift the soul to the other side.

At about 10:30 p.m., Anthony Largo of the Santa Rosa Reservation told the Luiseo singers to ready themselves. They would sing until dawn.

A short distance from the church, in the Cahuilla tribal hall, people sat at long tables to eat.

Feeding the people is part of the wake custom.

From big kettles simmering on a restaurant-sized stove, women ladled beef stew into serving bowls and set them out on the table. These were followed by bowls of beans and salad and canned peaches.

Between mouthfuls of stew and sips of hot coffee, the talk was warm and respectful.

Back in the church, Mark unsheathed his turtle-shell rattle, and the old songs resumed. And Rosie's journey continued.

Rest in peace with the ancestors, Rosie.

We Missed Some Grand Days under Uncle Erle's Oaks

JANUARY 16, 1996

I wish I could have been there, back in the days when Erle Stanley Gardner held court under the oaks of Rancho del Paisano with guests like mystery writer Raymond Chandler.

That must've been something.

Chandler, one of my favorite writers, used to live in La Jolla. Now and again, as did many writers and celebrities, he'd come out for a visit.

I see Chandler, author of such detective classics as *The Big Sleep* and *The Long Goodbye*, with round spectacles perched on his nose, reclining in a wrought-iron chaise lounge in front of the redwood lodge with a tall whiskey in one hand, an unfiltered cigarette in the other.

Not a big drinker, Uncle Erle (everybody called him Uncle Erle) probably sipped a short whiskey while pounding the chair arm with his free fist to emphasize his point.

Together, in the cool of a Temecula afternoon breeze, they might gripe about editors who couldn't leave a graceful sentence alone. Complain about accountants concealing royalties with smoke and mirrors. Compare notes on old sweethearts who dumped them for more promising catches, dandies with polished loafers and buffed fingernails.

If only I could have had one beer with them.

But I had never even set foot on the place until last Thursday afternoon, when I got lucky.

As the legend goes, Uncle Erle was just passing through in the late 1930s when he stopped the car to let his dog lift its leg. Lured by the scent of quail and rabbit, the dog bounded off to romp in the oaks, and Uncle Erle lit out after him. It was plain the dog liked it here. Turns out, Uncle Erle did too.

For more than thirty years, America's best-read author churned out Perry Mason books at the compound of houses, offices, guest cabins, stables, garages, and other outbuildings he called the "fiction factory."

Jeff Loefke, manager now for twenty years, agreed to take time from his farming chores to show me around.

According to Loefke, Uncle Erle bought five hundred and sixty acres from local Indians in about 1938 for fifty dollars an acre, a fair price at the time. Later Gardner would increase his holdings to one thousand acres, but he sold nearly half the ranch before he died in 1970. In 1975, Dr. Ed Boseker paid $1.5 million for the ranch. He has since bought more land, building it back up to eight hundred acres.

Loefke and I roamed the grounds. We passed a concrete-block bunker cut into the side of the hill.

"That's the root cellar," Loefke said. "Back then, the ranch was self-sufficient. They raised all their own food, even a small grove of Bartlett pears that were Uncle Erle's favorites," he said.

When Uncle Erle wasn't off fishing in the Pacific Northwest, or cruising in the Sacramento–San Joaquin River Delta in his houseboat, or hunting for lost mines in Baja, or staying at his other houses in Palm Springs and Idyllwild, he entertained a lot of guests who stayed in cabins at the Temecula spread.

The cabins have since been turned into rentals to help, along with the dry farming, to pay the ranch bills, Loefke said.

We kept walking. The buildings clustered under the shade of live oaks. One huge oak at the bottom of the wash has a circumference of more than seventeen feet. Dry leaves crackled underfoot.

Loefke pointed out Uncle Erle's lapidary room. Rocks he collected on his travels still sit in wooden bins near the door.

"Over there is where Uncle Erle's office was," Loefke said. "It's used for storage now."

His office has been recreated in the library of the University of Texas Library at Austin. You can look through a glass panel at his desk, at his artwork hanging from knotty pine walls, at his books on their shelves; punch a button and you hear Uncle Erle talk.

Loefke took me into the main lodge. The big kitchen had a woodburning stove, an electric stove, and a restaurant refrigerator with glass doors.

In the long living room, I sat on a rattan couch with leather-covered cushions where Erle Stanley Gardner once sat.

Then, I stepped into the small bedroom where he died.

My son's godmother, Juliana Rodriguez of Pala, kept house for Uncle Erle. She was there at his bedside when he died of prostate cancer at age eighty, in March of 1970.

"It was a sad day," she said.

A Surrealistic Juxtaposition
of Cultures

APRIL 3, 1996

Neon waves of blue and green cascade over the Fantasy Springs electronic billboard, flashing messages at passing drivers on Interstate 10: Caribbean stud poker...Live boxing...Las Vegas–style shows.

But Saturday night, my fourteen-year-old son, Brandon, and I bypass the casino glitz, the transplanted palms, the artificial water spouts, the promise of big pots, to take in the Cabazon Indian Reservation's Indian Powwow behind the casino.

Whenever I come here, I can't help but be dazzled by the contrasts—the head-on collision between old and new.

Not far from the Cabazon Indians' casino, archaeologists have unearthed Indian habitation sites thousands of years old.

Yet on this night, huge casino searchlights track the indigo sky, and in the narrow beams you can see nighthawks dart after airborne insects attracted by the light.

To celebrate local culture at this intertribal powwow, Tony Andreas, a Cahuilla Indian, emcees a performance of bird singers in the dance arena. A half-dozen groups, including Andreas's

Cahuilla bird singers, have shown up with gourd rattles in hand to sing and dance for the people.

Keith Mahone, forty-one, a Hualapai from Peach Springs, Arizona, stands before the microphone shaking a black-on-red gourd rattle to bird songs gifted to him by an elder when he was five years old.

His dancers—Sylvia Borchard, Lanadine Smith, Allene Smith, Goldie Coochwytewa, and her two daughters, Mignon and Omavensi, wear flowing satin dresses that Keith sewed from scratch.

The traditional designs on the dresses tell a story, Keith says.

Miss Teen Hualapai, Lanadine Smith, represents her tribe in a white satin dress decorated with patterns of green pine trees, "because we are the people of the tall pines," Keith says.

The women bird dancers do a kind of two-step, swaying back and forth like Rain Bird sprinklers to the ancient songs. Meanwhile, in the casino disco room, women in short black leather skirts, black spike heels, and black brassieres as outerwear dance hip-hop as the obligatory faceted mirror ball spits red dots onto the ceiling.

Yes, a night of contrasts.

Back at the powwow, the grand entry begins. More than four hundred dancers file into the arena—jingle dancers, fancy dancers, grass dancers, traditional dancers, and more—all in spectacular costumes.

They step to the thumping drums and high-pitched songs of Indians from the Plains. There are ten drums (groups that sing and play the drums) at this powwow. Blackstone, a well-known drum from Canada, bangs out a song. When Blackstone performs, other drummers and singers huddle around with tape recorders held high, trying to preserve the techniques for later study. As long as you're learning, you may as well learn from the best.

About a dozen men sit around the Blackstone drum, beating the drum skin with leather-wrapped batons. With their free hands, several pinch their throats to help reach the coyote-like high notes.

Across the parking lot from the powwow, Sandra Bernhard gives a concert in an open-air venue. Bernhard, best known for her lesbian character on *Roseanne,* wears a psychedelic, bell-bottomed bodysuit that glows red, green, and lavender as the gel lights change.

She does a blend of comedy and music backed by an all-female dance band called Fem2Fem. A strange kind of syncopation goes on as the Indian drums and the dance-band drums compete for the beat. As the Blackstone singers stretch their voices, Sandra belts out a campy version of "New York, New York."

As an Indian, I'm unsure about where this casino thing is taking us.

For instance, at the powwow I admired one dancer's costume of tanned buckskin, yellow and brown beadwork, leather shield, and staff topped with an eagle claw.

Then, while checking out the casino gaming room, I saw an Indian guy in black slacks, black silk shirt, black patent-leather slip-ons, white silk tie, and white sports jacket with a black handkerchief folded into the pocket. He looked like a Vegas pit boss.

It's a whole new look for Indians, I'll say that. But it takes getting used to.

Cowboy Was Content with a Simple Life

DECEMBER 11, 1996

He wore a straw cowboy hat, the band stained with sweat, the brim bent uneven by countless handlings. When days turned cold, he pulled on a navy-blue sweatshirt. Otherwise, he wore a white T-shirt and jeans.

He wasn't a big man, maybe 5 foot 7. He wasn't a loud man, preferring quiet talk and soft laughter to the din. Nor was he a greedy or overly ambitious man, choosing the simple cowboy life over all others.

Day in and day out, Tommy Portillo tended to twenty-five or so head of cattle. He drove them from their makeshift corral of tree limbs and barbed wire in the dry river bottom of the Pala Indian Reservation to higher ground where they could feed on scrub brush and green undergrowth.

These were tough range cattle, the kind of cattle that could eat spiny cactus apples or paper off a tin can, or his straw hat if he left it about.

Like his cattle, Tommy's horse had no pretensions. This was no blue-blooded cow pony that could wheel on a dime or pirouette like a figure skater. This was pure workhorse, back bowed with too many burdens, head held low with nose to the grindstone.

His saddle, mended with baling wire, bore no fancy tooling, the stirrups held no glittery silver studs.

In the gray dawn, Tommy would walk the short distance from his house to his horse. Wherever Tommy went, a small pack of rez dogs followed. Two shepherd mixes would actually help with the herd, while the rest tagged along with feigned importance.

Before throwing on the saddle blanket, Tommy checked his horse's back for sores, burrs, or bites; he felt each leg for soundness. With stubby, working-man's fingers, he tightened the cinch and fixed the bit into the horse's mouth—cold steel against warm gums—and the horse would toss his head at the shock of it, snorting bursts of early-morning steam through flared nostrils. It was the same every morning.

Left boot in left stirrup, Tommy grabbed the horn and launched himself over the saddle, leather creaking with his weight.

And with an orange thumbnail of sun showing over the mountains to the east, Tommy eased the herd down the dirt road, across the river, and up into the hills. The two good dogs took up the herd's flanks, while the others chased rabbits or barked at shadows.

In slow motion they moseyed in a procession—cattle, cattle dogs, no-account dogs, and Tommy—through the willows and sycamores. Now and again Tommy might whistle at one of his dogs to keep an uppity calf in line. But other than a dog's bark or a steer's low, he worked in silence.

Sometimes, on my way back from hunting, I'd run into Tommy as he pushed his cattle into the backcountry. He'd stop his horse for a moment and we'd chat. If it was football season we'd discuss Notre Dame's latest great victory or foul defeat. In summer, he cheered for the Dodgers while I rooted for the Giants, so we'd banter good-naturedly about the superiority of our respective teams. Our meetings always ended with a wave and a smile.

Bad weather never discouraged Tommy. He kept a green poncho tied to the back of his saddle. Even in a downpour, you'd find him sitting atop his miserable horse, watching his cattle eat, with the rain spilling down the creased brim of his hat.

Tommy started with the cattle as a kid in the early 1930s. His dad, Florencio, was a cattleman, and brother Danny and half-brother Louie Nolasquez helped as well.

Florencio also officiated at Indian burials, marking where the grave would be dug, checking with a tape measure to see that it was deep enough, and making sure the sides were square.

After Florencio's death, Tommy assumed the role, and was always the first to arrive at the graveyard when there was digging to do. He supervised countless burials.

One day in 1983, while he and Danny hoed weeds in the Pala graveyard, Tommy's sixty-four-year-old heart convulsed with pain. He took little notice of it, though, and kept hoeing. The next one felled him, however, and he died soon after.

Some of the cattle were sold to pay for his funeral.

Food Theory Backed by Bulk of Evidence

December 18, 1996

Was a time, back in my bachelor days, when I could open the refrigerator and find only ice water, a jar of mustard, and half a block of commodity cheese.

It got so I learned to like commodity cheese dipped in mustard. I had no choice.

Many reservation Indians did and still do get commodities from the U.S. Department of Agriculture. They are both boon and bane to the people.

Once a month, a truck from the Southern California Tribal Chairmen's Association stops in front of the Cupa Cultural Center on the Pala Reservation to dole out cheese; canned butter; powdered milk and eggs; canned meats; bags of pinto beans, rice and macaroni; assorted canned fruits and vegetables; and peanut butter and various cereals—both hot and cold.

Eligible recipients, people with incomes below the federal poverty level, load their cars with boxes of "commods" and drive home knowing that no matter what else happens, they won't starve.

And that's good. The downside to commodities, however, is what Indians jokingly call "commod bod."

I have a theory about why so many Indians, myself included, end up as heavyweights. Before white contact, for thousands of years, Southern California Indians ate wild foods. Game such as deer, rabbit, and wood rat boiled or roasted over an open fire provided low-fat sources of protein.

Along with the meat, we ate weewish, a no-fat acorn pudding, and seeds parched with a hot rock, and fresh greens picked near water—again, all no-fat.

Historically, we had no major sources of fat or processed sugars. We also expended more energy to get our food. We couldn't just drive to the supermarket, we had to hunt and gather in the steep countryside, burning calories all the while.

I have no scientific studies to back me up on this, but it makes sense to me that we are genetically predisposed to a diet high in protein and low in fat and simple sugar—the diet we survived on for thousands of years.

Enter commodities.

Take commodity chopped meat, for instance. My guess is that this chopped meat is the feds' version of Spam. It looks a little like Spam and kind of resembles Spam in taste. While the commod cans aren't labeled with nutritional information, I gotta think it shares Spam's fat content.

In the old days, I remember cutting off a thick slab and frying it in a cast-iron pan bubbling with commodity butter. After flipping over the chopped-meat patty, I'd top it with commodity cheese. When the cheese melted, I'd slip the browned patty melt between two pieces of white bread that quickly got soggy with grease. Add a little ketchup, and voilà, a "rez burger," just oozing with fat and cholesterol.

And then there was the canned pork. Simply opening the can could make you fat. Chunks of pork, the other white meat, swam in gelatin and lard.

I used to roll dollops of the fat-saturated meat into corn tortillas and deep fry them in shortening for my own poor-boy version of carnitas.

I used the fat and gelatin left in the can to spice up the leftovers to feed the dogs. And the dogs would get fat.

The commodity beef was like no beef I've ever seen. It, too, swirled in fat, but I ate it. I'd fry it with diced onions, jalapeños, and peeled tomatoes, and eat it with beans and store-bought tortillas.

For breakfast, if I was lucky, I might have a real hen's egg to whip into the powdered eggs. If not, I'd try to improve the powdered eggs by adding bits of chopped meat and pretending it was nice country ham. I'd stir the mixture as it cooked, hoping for yellow, fluffy eggs, but always getting greenish, beady eggs instead.

I'd grate commodity cheese over the scrambled mess, wishing it was a round of imported Swiss and not a block of super-processed commodity cheese.

And it wasn't just me eating this way. Half the reservation subsisted on commodities.

And we joked about it. If a person spent too much time in the bathroom, suffering from constipation, someone would yell out, "Can I get you another slice of commodity cheese?"

And, years later, I'm still trying to shed my "commod bod."

Grandfather's Stories of Life Are Lasting Gifts

December 25, 1996

In my forty-five years, I have received many great Christmas gifts. There was the Daisy BB gun (modeled after the 1894 Winchester) I got when I was ten. The Roy Rogers cowboy boots that made me feel ten feet tall. The quick-draw Mattel Fanner-50 cap pistols with the tooled-leather holsters. My first transistor radio—a Silvertone from Sears. My first record player, a Mercury, with surprising fidelity. My sleeping bag with the goose-down insulation that kept me warm on camping trips. And many more.

Yes, Father Christmas has been kind to me.

But it was my grandfather who gifted me best.

My grandfather, Paul Magee, was a Cahuilla Indian from the Pechanga Indian Reservation near Temecula.

A thickset man, he lived in button-fly Levis, plaid flannel shirts, and a white Stetson cowboy hat.

Some called him handsome, but his left eye drooped a bit, his nose was prominent, and he sported a pencil-thin mustache that was, more often than not, trimmed unevenly.

Rather than mess with them, all of his teeth were pulled while he was still a young man—such was the state of dentistry for

Indians in his day—but he got along quite well without them. He could gum a well-done steak lickety-split, and whistle loud enough to call his dog. "So who needs teeth?" he'd ask. Later in life, he tried a set of store-bought dentures, but they only cramped his smile. He seldom wore them.

He didn't read well, and could barely write his name. But now and then, he'd put on his reading glasses, the ones mended with a copper wire that hooked over his ear, to study the newspaper. Mostly, though, he listened to the radio. He could sit under a tree for hours learning about the world through news and talk radio. He greatly preferred the radio to TV, and greatly preferred the outdoors to being shut in.

My grandfather liked coffee in the mornings. He stirred in sugar and canned milk, and slurped it hot from a thick mug.

For breakfast he often ate oatmeal, because "it sticks to your ribs," he'd say. Or when he behaved himself, my grandmother would cook him a big breakfast of fried eggs, beans, potatoes, bacon, and tortillas.

But many times he didn't behave himself, and got icy stares and cold silence from my grandmother with his morning coffee. He'd drink it with a shaky hand and wink a bloodshot eye at me.

For my grandfather was a drinking man. And his drinking ways were both blessing and curse to me.

As a child, many nights I would bury my head in the pillow with worry. I knew how bad he could get. I had seen him fall against concrete steps and bust his head open. Seen him hit the pavement face first. Seen him passed out in the weeds in the freezing cold. But I loved him, flaws and all.

As I got older, I would roam the reservation when he caroused to look for him. When I found him, usually out cold somewhere, I'd help him home.

"You should have just left him," my grandmother would say in disgust. But I knew she didn't mean it.

When he didn't drink, he was a kind man, but quiet. He kept to himself, splitting kindling, hoeing weeds, burning trash—all without saying much.

But when he drank, he liked to talk. And because I'd listen, he'd talk to me. And what wonderful stories I'd hear. Tales of prospecting for gold with his father in the desert mountains. Of hoop dancing at powwows, of drumming for dances, of breaking green horses at a big ranch, of hunting for big bucks, of pitching curve balls for St. Boniface's baseball team. His world filled me with awe.

My grandfather was a man of simple wisdom who instilled in me a sense of wonder. He taught me to look at life with a child's eye, to believe in astonishment, to treasure what I saw.

And though he's been dead nearly ten years now, I still think of him watching over me, and I wake up eager for the day's doings. My grandfather taught me to love life. And for that, I'm ever grateful.

Now, if I could just give that to my children this Christmas, I'd feel I'd done him proud.

Merry Christmas to you and yours.

Hankering for Hongos Leads to Humid Hike

JANUARY 29, 1997

A gray drizzle—enough to dampen, but not soak us—swirled in morning gusts.

Raindrops dangled like costume jewelry on prickly oak leaves, hesitated, then fell on winter grass below.

More drops dappled the swollen San Luis Rey River, as muddy currents frothed around smooth stones and cottonwood snags.

My buddy Jean Jackson and I hiked the trail that followed the river's banks.

"Once I spotted several deer feeding at the base of that hill over there," Jean said. "I picked out a good spike, and dropped it right where it stood. The river was running strong that day, and I was carrying the deer around my shoulders, when I lost my footing and was swept under. The water was cold, real cold. And I couldn't get the deer off me. I practically drowned. Danged deer almost got his revenge."

We stopped for a moment to inspect a tree, a rough-barked willow, quite nearly dead. We scanned it from trunk to high branches.

"Nope, none on this one," I said.

When the elements converge just right, when brilliant sun follows heavy rain, when patches on a certain kind of willow get proper exposure, when damp warmth turns these patches into incubators, nature conspires to serve up a most delicious treat.

On the rez, we call them *hongos*, the Spanish word for mushrooms, but more correctly, they are a tree fungus called *saqapish* in Indian. I have no idea what they're called in English, but they can grow to the size of a pork roast, and rival French truffles in texture and taste.

I had a powerful hankering for some. So we hunted them along the river bottom just upstream from the Pala Indian Reservation.

"Years ago, there used to be a stray—part Lab, the rest dog— that stayed under that oak tree," Jean said, nodding his head toward an oak with branches that brushed the ground. "I used to feed it coyote and bobcat carcasses left over from trapping. Don't know what happened to the dog. Came one day and it was gone. Never saw it again."

This land holds many memories for Jean, who has trapped and hunted these hills since coming here shortly after World War II. Now seventy-eight, Jean has an arthritic knee that gives him fits in the cold and the wet. We took our time.

We passed a low, flat granite boulder bearing milling depressions where Luiseño Indians long ago used a pestle to pound acorns into flour for a mush called *weewish*.

I figured Indians poked along these same banks looking for hongos, too. The hongos would certainly enliven an otherwise bland weewish breakfast.

When she was alive, my grandmother always got happy when I brought home hongos. She loved them. She'd slice them thick and fry them up in bacon grease with onions, garlic, and red chilies. We'd eat them like meat, with fresh boiled beans and homemade tortillas.

I wished for hongos even more just recalling that.

We eyed another small cluster of willow trees ahead. As we approached we noticed a deadfall. The trunk where the bark had rotted off boasted a colony of small hongos. Too small to pick, though.

"We'll come back for those in a couple of days," I said.

"If we get enough sun, they should pop up," Jean said.

Rain clouds, blackened by bad intentions, rolled across the sky. A covey of valley quail scrambled in the winter-green underbrush and the leaf mold crackled under their feet. As we got closer, they exploded into the air, stubby wings a blur.

"Back in the late forties a black guy built a small shack downriver a piece and raised some pigs. He stuck it out for a couple of years, but he pulled out. It was a tough life," Jean said.

We wandered a bit more, but the hongos proved elusive. We returned to the truck, our gunny sacks empty.

"We'll come back," I said.

"Maybe the next day we'll be lucky," Jean said.

Voices of Past Resound amid Adobes of Cupa

FEBRUARY 26, 1997

A quarter-century ago or so, I sat in an adobe classroom, listening to Roscinda Nolasquez's patient voice, trying to hear the inflections, the accents, the gutturals of the Cupa language she taught.

From the front of the class she peered at us through thick glasses; hair, the color of bleached river rock, pulled back into a knot; fingers, gnarled by work, grasping a walking cane; long skirts gathered about her ankles.

She did her best to teach me, but I was a poor student. At the time, chasing other skirts had higher priority, I'm afraid.

Last week, I heard her voice again as I drove with her great-grandson Leroy Miranda Jr. through cattle country along Lake Henshaw in north San Diego County.

Leroy had brought a tape of her talking about *tatawila* dancers, men in eagle-feather skirts and owl-feather headdresses whirling around the fire.

It was good to hear her voice again.

Leroy and I were on a pilgrimage of sorts to Cupa, our ancestral village at Warner Hot Springs.

A lifelong student of Cupa ways, he pointed out features in the landscape that his great-grandmother and others had told him about.

"There is a place up along those rocks where footprints of the Little People climb up a rock face," he said.

He pointed to a mushroom-shaped rock: "That is Wind Rock, an evil place. Never touch that rock," he warned.

His education started when he was about ten, writing in big capital letters on foolscap the Cupa, or Cupeño, words Roscinda taught him. Now curator of the Cupa Cultural Center in Pala, he's been at it ever since.

Roscinda, born and reared in the village of Cupa, was a treasure of language and traditions. Many of her teachings can be found in a book called *Mulu'wetam: The First People* by Jane H. Hill, published by the Malki Museum on the Morongo Reservation.

When we got to Cupa, we first stopped, as is Leroy's custom, at the Chapel of St. Francis, a small adobe church built by the Cupas in 1830. Although sagging with age, the same adobes and hand-hewed rafters hold up the church. Priests from Santa Ysabel still say Mass there.

Then we visited the old cemetery behind the church to pay respects. Simple wooden crosses marked most of the graves. Susanne Blacktooth, 1892–1968, had a marble headstone, as did Ben Joseph Hyde, 1887–1961.

Roscinda's headstone—1892–1987—had her picture on it.

Just to the north of Roscinda's grave rest Taylor family members.

As part of our trip, Leroy had brought along old photographs he wanted to show Banning Taylor of the Los Coyotes Reservation, just north of Warner Springs.

Banning's wife, Nelda, greeted us at the door of their hundred-year-old adobe-and-wood ranch house. A big cast-iron kitchen wood stove warmed the place.

Banning, ninety-two, reclined in a chair. In his heyday, Banning was an artful politician. A dogged supporter of Indian affairs, he dedicated himself to arm-wrestling the government into living up to its treaty obligations. He served fifty-five years as tribal chairman.

He grew up in the historic Warner's Ranch house, and spent the rest of his life in the mountains of Los Coyotes, chasing cattle. He still runs about thirty head on reservation pastures, but mostly his son Frank tends to them now.

"Guess what I've been making," Nelda said. Banning and Nelda have been mates for sixty-six years. "Sixty-six years of Sing-Sing," jokes Banning.

"Pinole," she said. To make pinole she toasts wheat kernels in a cast-iron frying pan until they puff. "We used to have to grind it by hand, but Banning bought me an electric grinder."

She spooned pinole, ground into a fine powder, into a mug and added half-and-half and sugar. It was excellent. Tasted a little like Sugar Smacks.

"My son eats pinole when he knows he's going to spend all day in the saddle. Keeps him full," she said.

Pinole—a little taste of Indian Country.

As Always, Wally Leads the Way

July 2, 1997

Some twenty years ago, Shindig and Duke ruled Pala. When they swaggered down reservation roads, other dogs cowered on porches or barked safely from behind fences. Shindig was mostly bluetick hound, stocky and well-muscled. Duke was mostly German shepherd, tall and razor-blade thin.

Shindig and Duke, both scarred by countless battles, led the pack.

Duke was Wally Smith's dog. Wally led the pack, too.

In the old days, you'd find Wally parked at softball games leaning against his Ford pickup, bottle of Coors in hand, holding court with the rest of the boys. He had an ice chest, bigger than a bathtub, where the beer never ran out and the stories never ended.

Wally had the quickest wit of anyone I ever knew. People gravitated toward his pickup because that was where the laughter was. And the trouble, too. He didn't give a damn about political correctness. Sometimes, he liked to kick up the dust.

Once at a Rincon Reservation fiesta, back when it was held at the old fiesta grounds, I stood at a ramada, a willow-covered food booth, and ate a combo burrito—beans and hamburger on a homemade tortilla spiced with plenty of hot salsa.

It was between times. The dance and peon games hadn't started, but the ball games had ended. Not much going on. Soon an engine roared in the distance and dust exploded on the grassless ball field. Emerging from the dust clouds was Wally's old Ford, engine gunned, tires spinning doughnuts. Round and round he slid, dust rooster-tailing behind him. A brave thing to do, considering it wasn't his reservation. But leave it to Wally to give people something to talk about.

Wally seemed most at home behind the wheel. In a different world, he would have been a first-class race driver. You had to brace yourself for road trips with Wally. He had a heavy foot and drove with guts. With one hand on the steering wheel, doing ninety miles per hour through turns, he challenged death with ultimate calm.

More than once, my toes clawed into floorboard when he brodied into a curve. But you didn't show fear in front of Wally. Not unless you wanted to get teased for the rest of your life. You knew the risks when you stepped into his car. If you didn't want danger, you rode with somebody else.

As good a driver as Wally was, he wrecked several times. He was as scarred as his dog from car crashes, but it didn't deter him. He was just that way: hardheaded.

Starting when I was about eighteen, I worked summers on the Pala fire crew with Wally as my boss. Attached to the Cleveland National Forest, the federal job paid the same if we worked hard or hardly worked. But Wally pushed us. Sometimes, we would get into competitions, cutting brush for firebreaks. Another crew would be on a hill to the side of us and Wally would sweat us to beat them to the top. He'd take the lead, swinging a brush hook. He hooked with pride, filling us with pride, too, and we'd bust a gut to win. That night, when we returned to fire camp, we walked with our heads up. We heard other crews say, "You don't want to mess with Indian crews. They can hump it." That was Wally's doing.

Years later, as director of the Pala Avocado Project, I would be Wally's boss. His boss on paper, that is. Nobody was ever really

Wally's boss. He was his own man. But if you needed a favor, you could ask Wally. In many ways, he was bighearted.

For most of his life, he worked for the tribe, taking care of the water system, grading roads, maintaining the dump. He could have made more money elsewhere, but he liked the reservation. On the rez, he could do things his way.

Even when he got diabetes about three years ago, he refused to change at first. His doctors, his daughters, his ex-wife Cecelia warned him.

Piece by piece, the diabetes gnawed at him. First his toes. Then a foot. Then his fingers. Then his kidneys. Reluctantly, he stopped the beer and the wild life, but it was too late.

I visited him a couple of weeks ago. Always a fighter, he lay in bed, fighting to stay alive. I thanked him for the good times we had. Thanked him for teaching me to be Indian.

He died Saturday, at age fifty-eight. Once again, leading the way.

Mother's Love Endures, Even in a Heat Wave

SEPTEMBER 17, 1997

I sat on a patio chair in the back-porch shade, out of the sultry heat that beat down on my lawn like a funeral dirge.

Even in the shade, sweat trickled down my face and back. My dogs sprawled on the concrete, sighing in their sleep.

The water in the wading pool where just a couple of days ago my granddaughter had splashed and giggled languished against the blue vinyl walls.

A brown-and-yellow hornet floated on the surface, its transparent wings spread out like chapel windows in the dead calm.

I cupped my hand and scooped the hornet out onto the ground, knowing that the red ants would soon piece it out, then returned to the chair to stare again at the spiritless water.

It took me back to when I was about six, playing in our kiddie pool with my little sister and baby brother.

We were in a heat wave. All the adults talked about it. Mercury topping one hundred, relief nowhere in sight.

As we kids played, my mother lugged a laundry basket full of wet clothes out to the clothesline. She wore an apron over her loose housedress, the kind of apron with front pockets for clothespins.

I watched her stoop for a diaper, shake it out, then pin it to the line. She stooped for another, shook it, and pinned it too. Stoop, shake, pin, over and over, until the basket emptied.

I watched as she kneaded a kink in her back. She was nine months pregnant with her fourth child. Carrying a nearly ten-pound boy, my brother Kenny, her belly was huge.

On her way back, she stopped for a rest. With a groan, she lowered herself into a straight-back chair to watch us for a moment.

My mom wore zoris on her feet. They were bought, no doubt, at a drugstore sale for fifty-nine cents or so. I noticed her feet. She had Indian feet, dark and toughened by years of walking the dirt roads of the Pala Indian Reservation, where she was born.

But I had never seen her feet look so bad. They were swollen beyond belief. Her toes looked like sausages packed too tight. The flesh of her ankles threatened to break through the skin.

I remember gulping back a powerful sadness for my mother. I wanted to do something to comfort her. So I went to the galvanized washtub at the side of the house and filled it with cool water from the hose. Too heavy to carry, I dragged it over to her.

"Here, put your feet in this," I told her.

"Ah," she said, wriggling her toes. Then I motioned her to hand me a foot. I took it in my hands and rubbed it. I could see the flesh go momentarily white where I pressed

"Oh, thank you, son, that feels so good," she said, lavishing me with praise. I filled with pride that I could help.

Soon she got up, grabbed the laundry basket, and went back into the house. It wasn't long before we heard the clank of a metal spoon against the stainless steel pitcher.

That sound could mean only one thing: Kool-Aid. We rushed into the house like cats that hear the can opener. On the table, she had set out a plateful of saltine crackers spread with crunchy peanut butter. One by one, she poured Kool-Aid into Tupperware tumblers filled with ice.

And we ate, washing down the peanut butter that stuck to our mouths with the taste of artificial grape. Finished, we ran out to the pool again, leaving my mother to wipe up the crumbs and rinse the glasses.

With no air conditioning back then, she stood in front of the open kitchen window hoping for a breeze as she cleaned string beans, peeled potatoes, and worked hamburger into meatloaf for dinner.

That night, as I wrestled with the sheets to find a cool spot on the bed, I heard gasps of pain coming from my parents' room. Then I heard my father phone a neighbor lady to come watch us.

As my parents walked past my bedroom, I saw my mother in her quilted robe, carrying an overnight bag.

She left without saying a word to us. She wouldn't want us to worry. I worried anyway and prayed that everything would go all right.

God must have listened.

A Pouch Full of More Memories
for Mother

I'm sending you this medicine pouch for Christmas. It may seem an odd gift, since Indians from out our way weren't really medicine-pouch people, but I decided to send it anyway.

Here's why.

I first spotted the medicine pouch behind the glass counter in the Pala Store about six months ago. I'd pass by it, admire its design and colors, and think about buying it for myself. But always, I balked at the price.

Then as Christmas approached, I wondered what kind of gift you might like. Oh, I knew you'd like diamonds from Tiffany's, but I kept casting about for something in my price range.

My mind kept drifting to the medicine pouch.

You don't know it, but when I'm in the sweat lodge and the heat is intense and the sweat drips down my body, I pray for you and Dad. I pray the Creator watches over you, protects you from harm, grants you well-being.

Mom, you have done so much in your life to make my life better—all the cooked meals, the washed clothes, the Band-Aids on cuts, the drives to ball practice, the great Christmases of my youth.

But more than that, you have never failed to make me feel loved. No matter what I've done or said, you have always been in my corner. For that, I'm forever grateful.

I think about these things while I'm in the sweat (and other times, too, of course, but especially in the sweat). And I figured the medicine pouch might be a way to pass along some of these feelings to you.

So I'm putting things into this medicine pouch that matter to me, and I hope mean something to you. And I give them to you as a son gives something to his mother.

Awhile back, I roamed the hills near the cemetery behind the chapel at Cupa in Warner Springs. I followed dirt paths through the brush and the scrub oak, and I got a feeling about our people who walked these same trails. I felt connected.

For thousands of years, our people ate, bathed, and prayed there. The earth there is darkened by their blood, sweat, and tears.

As I walked I spotted pottery shards poking through the soil. I picked up several and felt the gritty heft of them in my hand. I knew they were from cooking pots and water jugs and ceremonial bowls, and I felt like I was holding pieces of living history, tangible remains of our people's lives.

I'm putting one of these shards into your medicine pouch, so that you will always have the ancestors with you.

For years now, I have had a special kinship with white sage. Before I sweat and before I play peon, I smudge with sage. To me it smells of mystery, of nature's secrets, of primordial powers. When dried sage glows red with fire, I'm soothed, sometimes even transported.

I've been told the sage smoke forms a barrier against evil. In the old days, when peon players played with medicine, and harm could result, players protected themselves against evildoers with sage. Do I, a college-educated man, believe in this? Yes. For I know sage has helped me.

When I jog the backcountry, and my muscles ache and my energies dwindle, I often pluck a couple of sage leaves, crush them between my fingers, and inhale their pungency. And I'm revived. I think of the light-footed Indians who once ran these paths, and I'm energized.

When my children cried out at night with bad dreams, I burned sage in their bedrooms and prayed for their peace of mind. And they would be comforted and sleep soundly from then on.

I look upon sage as a benefactor. So I'm putting some Pala sage into your medicine pouch, along with my prayers that it will protect you, and remind you wherever you go of the hills you grew up in.

I'm wrapping the sage in cloth from the black bandana that our peon team wore when Therman McCormick, our teacher, died more than a decade ago. I saved that bandana and wore it often around my neck while playing peon. It is a piece of my life that I give to you.

I also saved Gramps's Stetson cowboy hat. The one you bought for him so many years ago. It's old, beat-up, and moth-eaten now, but he wore it with pride. I still remember how his bearing changed whenever he put it on. He seemed to stand a little taller and life was grander for him in the shade of its brim. I loved your father, my grandfather. As I know you did. So I've clipped a bit of his hat so you can have him with you, too.

At the rear corner of Gram and Gramps's adobe house, there grows a great, red-flowered shrub that I can't name. Early one morning, Gram was out in the yard, pruning the shrub with a pair of hedge clippers.

She wore a white sweater against the early morning chill. And she worked slowly and carefully, trying to shape the bush into an aesthetically pleasing curve. We talked that morning, and she told me that it was her favorite plant. And she gave me some seeds so I could have its progeny in my yard.

Well, you know how much of a gardener I am. I never did plant any of the seeds, but I saved them. So I'm putting a seed into your medicine pouch so you can have a bit of the plant your mother, my grandmother, loved.

I think you're getting the point. I hope you'll carry this medicine pouch with you, and every now and then run your fingers along the beadwork and think of me, your son, and how our lives intertwine.

I give this to you as a son gives something to his mother.

With all my love this Christmas,
Gordon

Making Friends during College Orientation

Shortly before I left for college, my grandfather reached into the watch pocket of his baggy jeans, fished out a turquoise ring, and sheepishly handed it to me, as if embarrassed by the gesture.

A silver snake coiled around the ring's setting, its hollow-eyed head poised above the blue-green stone. I knew my grandfather must have found the ring while sweeping up at his janitor's job at the Catholic school. He couldn't have bought it. He never had any money. My grandmother saw to that because if he had money, he wouldn't have it long. He loved to drink, and he was happiest when buying drinks for his friends.

I put the ring on my finger. It fit like it was made for me. In appreciation, I put my hand out to shake his. My grandfather always shook hands the old Indian way, with the barest of touches. A gentle handshake was a sign of respect. Too strong a grip signified aggression. My grandfather was a gentleman.

A week before I was to start classes at the University of California at Santa Cruz, the school held a weeklong orientation for EOP students—that is, students enrolled in the Educational Opportunity Programs.

About a half-dozen Indians showed up, including me. We shared dorms with fifty or so black, Chicano, Asian, and other minority attendees. I worried about meeting Indians from other places. I wondered if Indians from outside my circle would be different. I needn't have worried. I have since found Indians are Indians all over. There's a shared culture. Crack a joke about "Indian time" or "going back to the blanket," and even a Cree from Canada laughs.

We became instant friends. There was Frank from a small rancheria in the Willits area. He was older, maybe in his mid-forties. He smoked Pall Malls one after the other, but only had one lung. He'd lost the other in a knife fight.

Frank was cool, though. Plus he had a car, a beat-up heap of an Indian car, but it ran. So Frank was my friend.

Frank knew Alan from before college. Alan was thin and quiet and kind of serious. He wore plaid cowboy shirts and two-toned Tony Lama boots.

I think Bill was from Mendocino County. His hair fell to the small of his back, straight and crow black. He didn't smoke, drink, or party. He ate health foods like alfalfa sprouts and tofu, and every morning he drank a godawful mix of brewer's yeast stirred into buttermilk. He was the poet of the group. You'd see him, his back propped against the trunk of a redwood tree, scratching out poems on scrap paper. Later, he'd copy them into his composition notebook with a fountain pen. He showed me his poetry. It evoked stark reservation images—fistfights, broken wine bottles, hungry children—that I found unsettling.

I didn't know Mary well. An Inuit with thick, black-framed glasses, she flew in late from Alaska. She seemed to keep the rest of us at arm's length, so none of us knew her well. Back then, we pegged her as stuck-up. But maybe she was just a bit shy.

Last, there was Sally. She was older, about twenty-eight, and an artist. She lived in the Santa Cruz area prior to attending the university, and had a cabin in Boulder Creek. Several Santa Cruz galleries hung her paintings and basketwork. An urban Indian, she had escaped from an abusive marriage to return to college.

Sally and I palled around for a time, but the wounds from her marriage ran too deep for us to get very close.

The early 1970s, before disco sucked the life out of the decade, brimmed with excitement, especially for a young Indian guy learning about the Indian world. I attended all-Indian conferences, sat on panels where we discussed Indian identity, argued with Bureau of Indian Affairs officials over self-determination, and drank coffee late into the night with American Indian Movement members.

For too long, Indians had taken what had been dished out to them. Not that I was a huge radical or anything, but I felt part of a movement that tried to correct some wrongs.

It was a big part of my education, a part I'm still proud of. Through it all, I wore my grandfather's ring. I can't wear the ring anymore, though. My fingers got too fat.

Dishing Out Advice: A Hazard of Getting Older

FEBRUARY 5, 1998

The older I get the more I seem compelled to dish out advice to the young, as if my supposed acquired wisdom is a confection, a lip-smacking treat they should be pleased to receive.

Usually my advice is couched in stories of my younger, hipper days. I'll be sitting around a table populated with twenty-somethings when some kind of irresistible force grabs hold and before I know it, I'm regaling them ad nauseam with tales from the sixties.

Usually my stories begin with, "When you get to be my age you'll find..." or "Back when I was your age..." or "You guys have it easy compared to what we had back in my days. Why..."

I mean, I know better. I should keep my trap shut. When I was twenty I didn't want some forty-six-year-old blowhard telling me about the wild times he had swing dancing to the Glenn Miller Orchestra.

I can remember rolling my eyes and stifling yawns while a potbellied fogey reminisced in full flush about the fuzzy pink sweater Molly Sue wore the night of their prom.

Now I have the potbelly and I'm telling the stories. But living in the past seems to be the curse of old age. And it doesn't look like I'm going to escape its spell.

Most of us won't. I gotta believe Baby Boomers will be horrible bores, even worse than the World War II generation.

You see, deep down in the heart of the Baby Boomer there is the solemn, unshakable belief that we are the most enlightened generation ever to walk this planet.

We grew up in the sixties, when idealism reigned. Ours was a generation of thinkers. We embraced radical ideas. We hallucinated into unexplored worlds. We believed in nature. We rebelled against power brokers. We tasted freedom. Our women burned their bras, for criminy sakes. How much freer could you get?

I can actually remember sitting in a coffeehouse with friends, drinking French roast, smoking Gitane cigarettes, and deriding the use of underarm deodorant as a crime against nature.

We'd say it was just another gray-flannel scheme to bilk the public. Corporate pigs conning us into believing we needed this roll-on or that spray deodorant so our body odors wouldn't offend. Then we'd say that as humans it is our nature to emit smells. It's natural. The odor is part of the way we fit into the order of the universe. Anyone who uses deodorant is a corporate dupe. Yes, really very plastic.

Similar conversations spewed forth on every college campus in America.

Weird. Yes. But we thought we knew what we were talking about. You see, we read back then. Late into the night, with jasmine incense burning, we sipped green tea and read Alan Watts, Hermann Hesse, John Fowles, J. R. R. Tolkien and Carl Jung, with the Rolling Stones playing on reel-to-reel tape in the background.

And their ideas made us feel above it all. Better than the rest. Turned us into sprout-eating, earth-shoe-wearing, wheat-bread-baking, astral-projecting space cowboys. But what did it get us? What did we do with all this information? Where are we now?

You'll find most of us nestled deep into our Barcaloungers, remote control in hand, watching our wide-screen TVs, making snide remarks to our kids about what simpering idiots the Gen-Xers on *Friends* are, and how much cooler we were at that age.

It galls me, sometimes, to see what we've become—crass consumers.

What happened to our ideals? What happened to the antimaterialism we preached?

I'm no better. I spend way too much time daydreaming about driving a showroom-new, four-wheel drive, king-cab pickup with a bruiser engine, brushed aluminum rims, and a matching camper shell.

There was a time when I would have thought such a pickup a gas-guzzling environmental nightmare. Now I'm wondering how many speakers for the CD player I can cram into the cab.

Somehow I feel I've let myself down. I feel self-deflated. And I get a queasy feeling of guilt when I start drumming my chest to the kids about how great things were in the sixties.

I'm better off just keeping the old trap shut.

New Pechanga, Old Bluesman
Hit High Notes

MARCH 5, 1998

One Sunday, some thirty years ago, I drove my grandfather to a tribal council meeting in the old Pechanga Indian Reservation schoolhouse.

On the way, he told me how in winter he walked to school in Pechanga with frost-cracked feet because he was too poor for shoes. How he carried a little lunch, maybe a bean tortilla roll and a hard-boiled egg, in a lard pail. How the boys sneaked up to the school's outhouse and peeked at the girls through knotholes. How they ripped up a Sears catalog for toilet paper, and how everyone hated the shiny pages.

Driving down the rutted dirt road toward the meeting, it didn't seem much had changed since his childhood. The sandy-bottomed reservation felt desolate, a place that knew hardships. Maybe a half-dozen families lived there, mostly in shacks thrown together with scrap lumber, then haphazardly added onto as families grew. Weeds, scrub brush, and cactus overran the yards where at least one rusted car or pickup sat up on blocks and several scrawny dogs slept in their shade.

Jobs were scarce in southwest Riverside County back then, and even when the people did work, the money wasn't good. Yet the Pechangas remained fiercely independent. Other reservations— Pala, Barona, Rincon—got federal funding for fancy tribal halls, paved roads, and basketball courts. But mistrustful of government, Pechanga turned its back.

Such was Pechanga thirty years ago.

That same year or maybe the year after, while attending high school in San Jose, I rode with friends to San Francisco's Avalon Ballroom to see a bluesman named Buddy Guy.

I'd heard of him before, but never really heard him. He stepped on stage in a sharkskin suit, a thin black tie, and a schoolboy grin, plugged in a Fender Stratocaster and changed my life.

He lit up the house with lightning-fast licks and slow, caressing blue notes. His hominy-grits-and-butter voice wooed and bellowed, cooed and called the pigs to supper. His music conjured the juke joints of Louisiana, where he grew up, then shifted into big-city riffs he learned with blues greats Muddy Waters, Willie Dixon, and Lightnin' Hopkins. Buddy Guy unhinged me.

Well, after a thirty-year wait, I finally saw Buddy Guy again Friday night in, of all places, Pechanga—at the Pechanga Entertainment Center.

Pechanga has changed since the sixties. Houses and double-wide mobile homes line dirt roads where cottontails once hopped. Shiny new trucks and cars are parked in driveways. The reservation has a new fire station, basketball courts, a ball field, a tribal hall, a health clinic, and more. Not all, but most of it, can be attributed to casino income.

Now, I'm not a gambler and I don't advocate gambling, but it's good to see prosperity on an Indian reservation. Indian people have paid their dues.

Back to Buddy Guy.

He headlined at Pechanga, along with John Lee Hooker, at the Art of the Beat Blues Fest, a fund-raiser for Temecula Valley Arts Council children's programs. Rob Anderson and Ginger

Greaves, two event organizers, helped arrange an interview for me.

After a short backstage wait, I heard a long white Lincoln limo whisper to a stop, and out stepped Buddy in a black overcoat and blue-striped overalls.

Security ushered me into a backstage trailer. Buddy, relaxing on a couch, smiled a welcome and shook my hand. Then we talked as friends do. We shared laments over the recent death of Buddy's longtime partner, Junior Wells, one of bluesdom's great harmonica players.

"It's scary, how all my friends are dying," he said. And as if passing the torch, he encouraged the young blues players to stick with it. We chatted some more, but I soon left him to get ready for his gig. I left thinking, "Now there's class."

Ask any one of the twelve hundred or so who saw him that night and they'll tell you: "Awesome…flawless…outtasight."

And it happened in Pechanga. Nobody, but nobody, saw this coming thirty years ago.

Last of Great Brush Poppers Rides Sober Trail

MAY 28, 1998

Nothing riles a cattleman like an open gate. Near the Santa Rosa Indian Reservation, about twenty miles east of Anza, George Tortes cusses under his breath as he pulls off to the side of Highway 74 to wire one shut.

"It was my dream to run a big herd up here. But how can you keep cattle from getting run over if people won't close the damn gates?" he says.

George, seventy-two, watches one of his Texas longhorns nibble some rain-fed grass and, as is his habit, tugs on his long, graying goatee. He wears blue jeans, blue vest, a western-cut shirt with snaps instead of buttons, and Roper cowboy boots. A straw hat shades his eyes from the harsh mountain sun.

Tortes is the last of the Santa Rosa Mountain Brush Poppers, a group of cattlemen who rode the rugged terrain around Santa Rosa Mountain, chasing cattle through rocky ravines at speeds others thought crazy. Men like Jim Weliman, Art Guanche, Joe Guanche, Johnny Meyers, Ernie Arnaiz, Ed Arnaiz, Clarence Contreras, Hank Lichtwald, Calistro Tortes, and Calistro's son George all rode as Brush Poppers. Only George is still alive.

We turn right onto the reservation and are greeted by a sign: SANTA ROSA INDIAN RESERVATION. NO HUNTING, NO TRESPASSING, NO NOTHING.

George and his wife, Rosemary (better known by her nickname "Fats," although she isn't fat), live on the same property his parents lived on. The last of George's cow horses feeds on land where George's father once farmed melons, corn, and beans.

Tortes started chasing cattle on horseback when he was about five, riding to keep his dad's stock from going too far up into the canyons. He would have been better educated, he says, if he had spent more time with books than broncs.

But he learned cattle. "You get so you can read cattle, know where they're gonna go before they do. You pick your spot, and throw your rope into the opening where the cow will be. Catching a cow that way is a great feeling."

His Mom, a Subish from the La Jolla Indian Reservation, died when he was about seven. He found her gasping for breath on the floor of their small house. He ran, tears streaming from his eyes, through the brush for help. Felix Kline had a Model A Ford and drove George's mom to the Indian hospital in Soboba. George never saw his mother again.

A Paiute and Navajo Indian born at the Soboba hospital, George had been adopted by the childless Tortes couple. George knows nothing about his biological parents. He never needed to. He was happy as a Tortes.

All he ever wanted to do was cowboy. He cowboyed up until he joined the Navy in World War II. He couldn't cowboy aboard ship, so he settled for being the ship's cook.

After the war, he looked for cowboy work but had to settle for exercising racehorses at Santa Anita and Hollywood Parks. Built like a jockey—short, wiry, and strong—he enjoyed the dawn rides on swift horses.

Back then, he also liked to drink. He mostly drank for fun, but when he lost an infant son to what he considered bad doctoring, the drinking became a way to numb the pain. Too drunk to ride, he lost his racetrack jobs, so he and his wife moved back to the Santa Rosa Reservation.

But the drinking didn't stop. Finally, a screech of tires and crunch of metal forever changed his life. His four-year-old son died in a car wreck while they were returning home from an Oak Grove café. Yes, George had been drinking and driving. After the accident, he disappeared into the bottle, as if trying to take his own life. Following a dispute in Valle Vista, he wrangled away the arresting officer's gun, and came way too close to pulling the trigger on the cop. George had spun out of control. It was while in jail that he embraced sobriety. That was thirty-seven years ago. The start of a new trail for him.

He's been sober since. And tries to help others into sobriety.

Nobody would want to live with what he's had to live with all these years, he says.

The Land Was Buddy Jean's Grocery Store

JUNE 11, 1998

June gloom shrouded the porch in gray. Moisture beaded on the pointed tines of old deer antlers nailed to the wall. Coyote skins hanging from rafters were wet to the touch. Damp earth clung to the paws of the dogs, leaving smudged tracks on the concrete floor.

My buddy Jean Jackson sat in his heavily padded chair on his porch on the Pala Indian Reservation, sipping tea from a giant cup. I sat on the makeshift counter across from him, a favorite perch of mine for the last thirty or so years.

I love his stories.

You see, much of Jean's life has been a quest for cheap eats. He has been a lifelong hunter and a fisherman, not so much as a sportsman, but as a harvester of nature's offerings.

Most people drive to the grocery store, wheel their shopping cart past the refrigerated cases, and pick up a rump roast wrapped in plastic for Sunday dinner.

Not Jean. He'd rather fight his way through the brush with a bloody deer slung across his shoulders, secure in the knowledge that his hard-earned money won't be squandered on meat that month.

Now eighty, Jean can't get around like he used to. But there was a time he was one of the world's great walkers. In Idaho, where he was reared, it was nothing for him to pack in forty miles to his winter cabin with a seventy-pound grubstake on his back.

Even at age seventy, Jean was tireless. I used to traipse around the backcountry with him, and at nearly half his age I had trouble keeping up.

Most of that walking had to do with the gathering of free food. In the old days, you could open Jean's freezer and find plastic bags full of bluegill, venison steaks and sausage, skinned rabbits, lengths of rattlesnake, frozen ducks, and maybe a catfish or two.

Jean and his longtime mate, Mary Nejo, used to pick olives by the bucket and home-cure them. He had a curing brine that included onions, garlic, and other spices. I used to sit at his place and eat olives by the quart.

For a while, he raised ducks. You should have tasted his pickled duck eggs with salt and pepper and a sprinkle or two of Tabasco sauce. Mmmmm.

And his smoked bluegill were a big hit, too. Even the carp caught at the La Jolla River tasted decent, although bony.

Some of his concoctions weren't quite so successful. There was the wine he made from oranges picked from his tree. It tasted like sour cough syrup and played hell with the body. After a fruit jar of that stuff, some victims had to spend hours locked in Jean's outhouse.

And there was the elderberry wine that left the drinker with a hangover that felt like an ax buried handle-deep into the skull.

Many of Jean's adventures have started in pursuit of low-priced chow.

He likes to tell of the "Great Turkey Shoot." As most of you know, a turkey shoot is a rifle competition where crack shots test their skills at targets. The best shot wins a turkey.

But Jean's turkey shoot went a little differently. Most old-timers in the Temecula-Murrieta area remember Tony Ashman, a much-respected Pechanga Indian who was 102 years old when he died in 1980.

To make a little extra money, Tony raised turkeys from his ranch near the Pechanga Indian Reservation. He sold them pretty cheap.

This was back in 1948, when Jean first came to this part of the country. And as is Jean's nature, when he heard about the cheap birds, he cut a bargain with Tony.

Thanksgiving Eve, after knocking off his job as a concrete laborer at Vail Dam, Jean swung by Tony's ranch to pick up his turkey. He envisioned it plucked and dressed, ready for the oven.

But when he got to Tony's, Tony handed him an old single-shot .22 and pointed to a big turkey roosting in a tree.

Jean laughs when he tells it: "Yeah, I had to walk over and shoot that turkey out of the tree. No wonder it was so cheap."

Like I said, anything for cheap eats.

Barefoot on a Lark in Summer

AUGUST 20, 1998

When we were kids, we seldom wore shoes in the summer. The soles of my feet were so toughened I could play basketball barefooted or grind out a cigarette with my heel or cross the hot tarmac of Pala Mission Road without breaking into a sprint.

We didn't have TV or even a radio back then. But we did have the run of the reservation. And I remember those barefooted days of freedom as the best times of my life.

My cousin Randy Trujillo and I would often meet early in the morning when it was still cool. He lived with his parents and a passel of brothers and sisters in the small house behind my grandmother's. Sometimes I'd roust him out of bed and we'd wolf down a quick breakfast of white sugar on Wonder Bread and then let the screen door slam behind us.

Thus began our day's adventures.

Randy was about a year older than me and knew more about the mysteries of the rez. So I mainly followed his lead.

Being poor kids, getting a few coins in our pocket was often a priority. We'd pad along the backroads of Pala, our toes pasted with dust, looking for pop bottles. At the Pala Store we could get three cents a bottle. But finding any took luck. A couple of rez winos often patrolled at dawn for bottles, hoping to collect enough for a morning cure. They'd usually snatch all the easy pickings. We'd have to beat the bushes for ours.

Red ants were a problem for barefooted wanderers. Once I stepped on a busy hill and the ants attacked my feet. The bites burned like fire. I howled in pain, and my Uncle Peter, Randy's father, heard me.

"What's the matter, boy?" he asked.

"Those danged ants bit me."

"We'll fix 'em."

He went into the house and came out with a 12-gauge shotgun. He raised the scattergun to his shoulder and blasted a round of birdshot into the ant hill. Dirt and bits of ants flew everywhere.

Ah, sweet revenge.

With each of us carrying a brown bag loaded with bottles, Randy and I clinked as we walked. At the store, we'd buy a pop and some Bazooka bubble gum. We'd stick three or four pieces in our mouths and sit on the steps leading to the mission, blowing bubbles. When the bubbles exploded, the usual procedure was to take the wad out of your mouth and mop up the tendrils of pink gum stuck to nose, cheeks, and chin, then pop it back in for more chewing.

After our jaws began to ache, we'd spit out the gum and move on. Race Freeman lived close to the store. He had a nice, big loquat (we called it "low-cut") tree in his yard. Like cattle thieves, we'd case the joint from behind some bushes. Then if the coast was clear, we'd run to the tree and stuff as many loquats as we could reach into the pouches we'd made by holding out the bottom edges of our T-shirts.

Then we'd dash off, giggling with our plunder. Now, I'm sure Race would have given us all the loquats we wanted just for the asking, but the fruit seemed sweeter because it was stolen.

Jean Jackson had a nice pomegranate tree, and we'd loot that, too. Across the San Luis Rey River, the Ardilla brothers grew watermelons, red and juicy. But we were too scared to rip them off. We'd heard that the brothers were medicine men who'd witch us if we stole from them.

In the afternoons, with the sun on high, we'd go to my Aunt Martha's for Kool-Aid. We'd pour it into tin tumblers filled with ice and watch the condensation bead on the outside of the glasses.

Best of all, we'd all go rabbit hunting if my cousin Robert Banks, who was a few years older than us, was home.

We'd hunt the afternoon away, taking turns with the small .22 bolt-action rifle. To stave off thirst, we'd suck on pebbles to keep our mouths from drying out. Sometimes we'd cut cactus and suck the moisture out of the pads.

If the hunting was slow, we'd shoot Lucky Lager cans lined up on fences, using the red X on the can as the bullseye. Or, for a moving target, we'd plink at a hubcap thrown into the air.

We'd come straggling home around dark, and my grandmother would have dinner saved for me.

Then to bed. I could hardly wait for the next day to do it all over again.

Imagination Has Free Rein under the Stars

SEPTEMBER 17, 1998

In the old days, when I used to smoke, I often sat out back to gaze at the stars by the light of my glowing cigarette.

Now I'm smoke-free, but the habit of sitting out at night continues. Behind my old trailer, I settle into the wooden chair I rescued from a Sherman Indian High School dumpster a couple of years ago. Sans cigarette, I inhale lungfuls of fresh air and exhale worries, relaxing my muscles as I do.

Soon the sound of my breathing blends with the night chorus of crickets chirping from beneath deadwood and dogs barking at shadows and cars droning along the highway.

With my body leaden in the chair, I close my eyes and, as much as possible, untether my mind, giving it free rein to go anywhere it wants to.

Here are some of the places it travels:

The moon, cool and luminous, hovers above the indigo sea, leaving silvery tracks in the calm. Fishing boats, their masts standing like cowlicks against the horizon, tug gently against anchor lines.

I'm sitting in the moon's glow on the veranda of a small,

whitewashed Greek house. It's perched above the Aegean, on rocky cliffs where sea birds roost at night. I can hear the sea lap against the sand far below. And music drifts up from the tavern in the fishing village down the road. Now and then the men laugh, and I wonder if the joke was good.

By lamplight, I read Lawrence Durrell, who wrote books from a place much like this in Corfu. But he complained about writing while living on the island. Much too peaceful, he said.

As I read, warm breezes ruffle the pages and the lantern-flame jitterbugs for a moment, then quiets.

There is a platter of black olives and cheeses and strips of fresh pita bread on the table. Everything is drizzled with garlic-flavored olive oil. I bite into an olive, spit out the pit, then sip Athens beer from a thick glass. I look up to see a pod of dolphins cavorting in the sea, their sharp dorsal fins silhouetted in the moonlight. I watch them until they swim off into blackness. I return to my book, content.

In another of my travels, I brush the rain off my raincoat and hang it on the coat rack. I place my soaked felt hat atop it. The rain, full of itself, tap dances against the plate-glass front window. Inside, the windows fog with human warmth.

The storm hasn't dampened the Parisian sense of fun. A pianist, a hefty fellow in a blue suit, fingers speakeasy jazz on a piano with yellowing keys. Eyes closed, lips pursing to the blue notes, he knocks out licks that sway the night crowd.

A woman in black net stockings and a tight woolen dress sits drinking red wine and tapping her long, blood-red fingernails against the table top. Her man, natty in a sweater vest and sports coat, dangles a fat cigarette from his mouth and gestures wildly, flinging arms this way and that as he tells his story. She smiles at him.

Table-hoppers clot the spaces between tables. Whirling, overhead fans cut through the blue smoke, sending it dancing toward room corners. Conversation echoes like distant thunder in the close room.

A high, beveled mirror reflects rows of liquor bottles. The aproned bartender wipes up spilled beer with a towel. I edge sideways into an opening at the mahogany bar and order a vin rouge. The barkeep uncorks a bottle and splashes a dollop into a stemmed glass.

Light bulbs burn behind etched-glass coverings. Framed posters of high-kicking cancan dancers hang on the wall. A couple of whiskery absinthe drinkers sit at a table and glower into the depths of their glasses.

Toward the back of the room, revelers at a big round table huddle about an expressive, baritone-voiced man. The women laugh a little louder than necessary. The men seem reluctant to look him in the eye.

Ernest Hemingway, shirt collar unbuttoned, tie askew, holds court for his entourage. F. Scott Fitzgerald, eyes at half-mast, sits next to him.

Hemingway spots me. "Hey, Scotty, it's that bloke who wrote that damn good Indian novel." Hem says to me, "Come join us, won't you?"

I take a chair between Hemingway and Fitzgerald. And the night begins.

Morning Run Jogs Memories of Reservation

OCTOBER 15, 1998

Sunday morning, I waited until after *Sunday Morning* to run. Even without Charles Kuralt, *Sunday Morning* is my favorite TV show. More nourishing than champagne brunch, the combination of news and arts always enlightens and uplifts.

With the final credits rolling, I laced up my cross-trainers. Then I snapped off the TV and stepped out the trailer door. The grinning dogs wriggled in excited circles. I wished I could get so enthusiastic about exercise.

I decided on a long run that morning, and headed for the backcountry of the Pala Indian Reservation, across the San Luis Rey River.

In my slow, lumbering slog I passed the shaded front yard of my friend Bobby Lavato. Up in years, he often sits out front, watching the day go by. But this morning he wasn't to be seen. Once Bobby was a premiere athlete, with quickness, endurance, and power. Now he has trouble getting around. I wished him well. I thought about him as I ran, hoping the exercise would stave off my own decline. I kicked up my pace.

On this windless morning, the sycamores lining the dirt road stood in silence. But the trio of dogs at Jeff Ravago's place came to life as we neared. Jeff's dogs, a cross of German shepherd and rez mutt, barked with fur bristling behind their necks. Griz, ever the brave heart, positioned himself so that I was between him and the snarling dogs. That way, should they attack, I'd be first to get it. Griz will always know where the back door is in a bar fight.

I didn't see Jeff, either, but I recalled times thumping the heavy bag hanging in the living room of his old house. That, by the way, is my definition of a good living room. One with a heavy bag in it.

I could hear Mexican music—lilting accordions with a polka beat—coming from the trailer houses lined up next to the big concrete-block house of the cactus ranch, about twelve acres of commercially planted cactus. A couple of guys stood in the yard around a smoldering fire. One of them kicked at the coals with a sharp-toed Mexican cowboy boot. I see guys in those tall-heeled boots walking all over the place. Man, those boots would kill my feet. Mighty tough hombres, I'd say.

Further along, I waved to a woman in a white sweatshirt who picked tunas—red cactus apples—from a cactus cluster that spilled over a fence onto the shoulder of the road.

With tin foil bunched to protect her hand, she plucked the apples and dropped them into a plastic bucket.

My buddy, Wayne Nelson of the La Jolla Indian Reservation, told me the other day of a good way to remove the tiny cactus spines. Take a box, put apples in the bottom, cover with sand, and shake the box. The agitated sand will knock the spines off. Then take a knife and make three lengthwise cuts to peel the skin back. Put the peeled apples in the fridge and wait for them to get cold. Eat when tempted. Very good. Very sweet.

We veered off the main road and headed for the racetrack, a crisscrossing of tracks where reservation kids spin around on dirt bikes and three-wheelers. When we were teenagers, we'd light night fires back here, listen to Etta James, and drink beer. And there's an oak tree where we'd nail up targets to sight in our guns.

I can remember taking my son Brandon here. Too young to hold up a gun, Brandon sat in the pickup bed so he could rest the gun on the bed and take aim at the target. Even then he was a good shot.

Farther along the sandy trail, we passed the Eagle Lodge, a sweat house put up about four years ago for a group vision quest. I went four days without food or water here, sweating and praying every night. Quite an experience.

I jumped a running creek where the dogs laid in a pool and drank. The sun climbed higher and sweat collected beneath my hooded sweatshirt.

We turned up an old wagon trail that winds toward the reservation's southern boundary. But it was too overgrown with poison oak, so we turned around and headed home.

After about two and a half hours of running, we pulled into the Pala Store. I drank Diet Pepsi till it burned.

Rez Life Offers Indian Comics Abundant Tales

NOVEMBER 5, 1998

With the shadowy San Bernardino Mountains hulking in the background, red, yellow, and sky-blue neon lights fire up the night.

Even on a Sunday, the parking lot of the San Manuel Indian Bingo and Casino is jammed. Don't people have to work on Mondays anymore? I finally swing into an empty slot at the far end.

Fall chills the air. I could be at home, reading the Dr. Andrew Weil book next to my bed while listening to Latin jazz master Eddie Palmieri. Instead, I'm weaving my way through the casino crowd to the see the Native American Comedy Show.

I find the entrance to the bingo hall and head toward the front. The seating is first come, first served, but I'm early so I get a good seat.

I run into a contingent from the Pechanga Reservation, near Temecula, who have come for the show, and I stop to say hello. I notice other Indians in the crowd as well, and I take that as a good sign.

I sit on a swivel chair at a long blue bingo table. Soon the house lights dim, and Floyd "Red Crow" Westerman steps through red velvet curtains into the spotlight on the small stage.

I remember Westerman from the early 1970s, when he made a name for himself as an Indian activist and folk singer. Although still an activist, forever campaigning for Indian sovereignty, he is better known these days as an actor—in many TV roles and in movies, including *The Doors* and *Dances with Wolves*.

His silver hair pulled back into a ponytail, this warrior of many battles straps on his acoustic guitar, pulls up a stool, and sings his music in an unfaltering baritone.

"Going back to the land I love, where the skies are big above me. Leave me alone, can't you see I'm going home…"

"Back in the seventies, I thought maybe by the year 2000 once and for all we would all (Indian people) be sovereign nations," he says. He's still hoping.

Then Westerman introduces the first comedy act, Andrew "Drew" Lacapa.

Lacapa walks out on stage in a brightly colored, oversized shirt, shorts, and black, high-top tennis shoes. With short black hair and a goatee, he blinks at the crowd through Drew Carey–like, black-rimmed glasses.

"I'm three hundred pounds of love," he says. "I'm what happens when you eat commodities (government surplus food) for thirty-eight years."

A White Mountain Apache, he also has Hopi, Tewa, and Scotch-Irish blood flowing through his veins.

"I do want to stop for a moment to thank my Scotch-Irish ancestry for my (pause) alcoholism," he jokes.

A reservation Indian, Lacapa jokes about rez life. He talks about the aromas of the rez, especially the one coming from the outhouse. He talks about growing up not with powwow music but with soul tunes by Aretha Franklin, Marvin Gaye, James Brown.

It was his fantasy to scoot and groove, bump and grind to songs so hot you "want to sop them up like gravy," he says.

"Don't get me wrong. I'm a traditionalist, too. I'm not wearing any underwear."

Then he dons a blue Apache dress and does a hilarious bit about breaking out the big Tupperware bowl, the one you take to potlucks with your name written in fingernail polish on the bottom, to make tortillas for his kids.

Abel Silva, a descendent of the Juaneños from Mission San Juan Capistrano, follows Lacapa. Much of his act is done in mime—clever, physical routines acting out Indian legends with a modern spin, like hunting with a bow and arrow in olden times, then opening a can of Coca-Cola. It's one of those things where you just had to be there to get it.

Charlie Hill, an Oneida Indian from New York now living in Los Angeles, headlines the show. His graying hair is pulled back into a ponytail, too.

Brash and irreverent, Hill paces the stage, firing jokes, shooting from the hip. He's very funny.

"We're hoping Indian casinos make so much money that someday we're gonna be able to buy our land back—from the Japanese."

His delivery has me belly-laughing. I drive home, pleased that Indian humor is finally reaching wider audiences.

Aunt Inez, End of Era, Source of Rich Memories

JANUARY 14, 1999

In Pechanga, on the other side of the barbed wire fence, tall winter grasses sprouted from the damp earth. An ancient elderberry tree sent up a snarl of naked branches. A sky-high oak threw mottled shadows that shifted in the winds.

On this side of the barbed wire fence, the cemetery side, the dirt was scraped bare of weeds. More dirt was mounded at the side of the grave. And my Aunt Inez (Magee) Moss was in her casket, which was poised on cross members over the open pit.

I stood to the side and watched as attendants lifted the lid to her wood-grained casket. A golden cluster of oak leaves embroidered the beige satin lining. She would face that cluster for eternity.

Her silvery hair, thin with her eighty-eight years, puffed out on the pillow. Her eyes were tranquil beneath closed lids. Her hands gently crossed her chest.

Diamond rings sparkled from her thin, pointed fingers. Without the jewelry her hands resembled my grandfather's hands, and in some ways, my own hands.

She was my grandfather's last sibling. The last of a long ride. Once the Magees included Uncle Bobby, Uncle Freddy, my grandfather Paul, Uncle Raymond, Aunt Cecilia, and Aunt Inez. All of them were born in Pechanga, an Indian reservation south of Temecula. All of them lived out their lives not far from their birthplace.

And then there were none.

My Aunt Inez was born April 18, 1910. There's a picture of her at about age four on the funeral memorial card. She's sitting in a fancy wooden chair in a white lacy dress with a big white bow clipped to her black hair.

Even then her eyes seemed sad.

My Aunt Inez's mother, Mary Lubo, died shortly after that picture was taken. And my aunt grew up in boarding schools, first Sherman Indian Institute (now Sherman Indian High School) in Riverside, then St. Boniface in Banning.

She told me about the nights, about being scared in the dormitory rooms. How the strict nuns at St. Boniface had switched her for running loose in the hills behind the school, which were off limits. How the nuns knocked her against the wall for throwing bread in the cafeteria.

"I kept getting in trouble in school, but I was naughty," she said.

No matter how bad it got at school, it was better than home.

"I didn't even want to come home during the summers, my stepmother was so mean. I just hated it at home," she said.

I thought of these things, as the funeral crowd filed past her open casket to pay final respects. As Johnny Chutnicutt, Georgianna Viveros, Margaret Holley, and others sang the old funeral songs: "Adiós, Adiós, Adiós..." and "Santos, Santos" and "Amazing Grace" and "The Old Rugged Cross."

And her daughter, Dolores Calac, wiped tears from her eyes, and Dolores's son, Mark, put an arm around his mother's shoulder to console her.

When the time came, I grabbed a shovel, and scooped dirt from the mound, and threw it into her grave. I heard the dirt slapping against the casket lid. I heard the sobbing loved ones. I heard my breath quickening with exertion. I heard the solemn voices of the volunteer choir.

And there was a certain rhythm to it all—the digging, the crying, the breathing, the songs. A shaken-rattle cadence to the cycle of Indian life.

With the dirt piled high on her grave, the women placed flowers over her. And the flowers perfumed the cemetery air.

After the funeral, during the slow shuffle back to real life, I shook hands with people I hadn't seen in years. And I talked with cousins and other relations about Aunt Inez.

Most headed to the tribal senior center for the traditional post-funeral stew. But I rushed back to work.

Sunday night, in the sweat lodge, I prayed for Aunt Inez, and wished her a comfortable journey to the other side.

And I took a moment to recall the infectious laughter of Uncle Bobby. I saw Uncle Freddy's joke-hat that read "HOW." I felt my grandfather's gentle eyes. I chuckled at my Uncle Ray's senatorial ways. And I appreciated my Aunt Inez's subdued dignity.

I remembered them all, because it is our memories that keep the departed alive.

Six beloved Indians, and then there were none.

Good Intentions Still Blooming in the Garden

FEBRUARY 18, 1999

There was a time on the Pala Indian Reservation near Temecula where I live when life fell more in step with the seasons.

These days, most Pala people work off the reservation. Gone all day, they return at night to some beans and frybread for dinner, relax to some TV, then trudge off to bed.

Maybe they'll step out back to scrape leftover beans and gristle into the dogs' bowl, or carry garbage out to the trash cans, but little time is spent in the yard. People are too danged busy.

Back in the 1950s, when I was a kid summering with my grandmother, the reservation seemed slower-paced, and more self-contained. Few had gas money for the drive south to Escondido. Temecula was a dusty cowtown where a dog could nap undisturbed on Front Street, so there was little point in going up there.

Jobs were scarce for Indians, and people did things around their homes to put food on the table. Corn, tomatoes, and chilies grew in well-hoed rows. Chickens scratched amid the rows. Hogs sloshed in pens out back. People picked wild mushrooms and cactus apples and mustard greens to add variety to the menu.

There was a rhythm to the seasons. Spring planting, summer hoeing, fall wood-cutting, winter repairs.

Today, if the grass crackles underfoot with hoarfrost, you simply wear a jacket for the drive to work. If it's hot outside, well, you wear a short-sleeved shirt. No big deal.

Climate-controlled buildings further dilute the seasons. In most offices, you can't open a window, so the workday is spent in processed air. It's so artificial, it's like working in atmospheric Cheez Whiz. Stuck in a cubicle, you can't tell if it's winter or spring.

But the seasons do exist. My grandmother lived her life in seasonal rhythms. She picked lemons and squeezed fresh lemonade in summer. She gathered fresh mustard greens in the winter. She snapped off elderberry blossoms in the late spring, drying them for medicinal tea. But one season eluded her: planting season.

Every year, in late February, she'd talk about planting a garden.

She had a spot for her garden, a small plot of land just to the east of her adobe house. A carob tree shaded part of it, and the remainder got plenty of sun.

The soil was decent and a nearby faucet and hose stood ready for irrigating. All was in place.

In February, when the winter sun warmed the plot, she'd talk about how this year she was going to plant tomatoes, onions, and chilies for fresh salsa. And she was going to plant yellow corn, squash, and green beans. She loved green beans. Oh, and she wanted flowers, too.

But spring would come and go, and the planting season would pass her by, and nothing ever got planted.

I don't know what happened. She wasn't a lazy woman by any means. She worked around the house from before daylight to past nightfall on other projects. But somehow the garden never took shape.

For a time, my aunt's husband, Robert Hayes, kept a sheep tied to the fence in the garden plot. Coyotes or dogs had mauled the sheep, tearing off a piece of its face, so the owner just gave my uncle the animal. For a month or so, the sheep grazed in the garden, but the wound wouldn't heal, and finally Hayes dispatched it. The sheep did, however, leave behind good fertilizer that my grandmother never took advantage of.

Oh, she made starts. Some years, she raked the plot, and occasionally she got as far as spading the earth. I can still hear her singing badly out of tune while she worked. But the garden never came to be.

The other day I walked through the old garden plot. A few leathery pods cling to the near-dead carob tree. Gopher holes pock the landscape. Untamed grass and weeds prosper. Still no garden.

To my shame, I never helped her. Even when I was older, I was too busy swilling beer and chasing Indian girls to grab a shovel to make her dreams come true.

I wish to heck I had. But it's too late now.

And, like my grandmother, I too make empty garden promises. But this year, this year will be different. Maybe.

Young Writer: Best Way Is the Hemingway

MAY 20, 1999

When I was a young writer living in my grandmother's house on the Pala Indian Reservation, one problem was finding a place to write. I couldn't write in my room. I slept in a screened-in back porch with my Uncle Peanut. There was barely room there for our Army bunks and the water heater.

Certainly no place for the desk, bookshelves, and other trappings I envisioned a writer needing.

Besides, my Uncle Peanut's lifestyle didn't mesh with the writing life. Back then he was a wino. At three a.m. he'd be nipping his bottle and smoking a Kool. At five in the morning his buddies would bang on the door with offerings of peppermint schnapps. By the time I got up, I was dog tired from not sleeping.

Back then, I had never met a real writer, but I knew many had fine places to write. I used to check out books from the Pala bookmobile on my favorite writer, Ernest Hemingway, and had admired photos of his Cuban writing lair.

I read all of the famous scribe's works that I could get. I knew he often wrote dialogue standing up. But he also had a desk. And floor-to-ceiling bookcases. And stuffed African antelopes on the wall. Most of all, he had solitude. I envied Hemingway's solitude.

At my grandmother's house, if it wasn't my uncle bothering me, it was the nieces and nephews, who were always underfoot.

To try to get away, I set up my portable typewriter on the kitchen table. It was a ghastly table, a lime-green veneer on wobbly, cast-iron legs, but with the kitchen's doors closed, I could write there.

My young writer's eye danced with imagery for short stories and novels, but before I could finish typing a thought, my grandmother would shuffle in to bang some pots. When she couldn't think of something to talk about, which was seldom, she hummed. About the time she finished, my grandfather would take a coffee break from cleaning the yard and sit down and chat.

"Boy, Fernando must have tied one on last night," my grandfather would say with a small degree of envy. Fernando was one of his drinking buddies. "Did you hear him? He roared like a lion this morning."

Even back then, I wanted to be a famous writer. But to get famous, I had to write undisturbed.

I talked to my grandmother about needing a place to write. She suggested I go see Aunt Martha, who might have a room in her old house.

So I did. Shortly after World War II, the government gave away surplus military homes called Linda Vista homes. If Indian people had a mind to, they could go to San Diego, tear down a house, and reassemble it on the reservation.

But the homes were shoddily constructed. The plyboard was paper thin. The windows rattled and cracked in the wind.

The house behind my Aunt Martha's was a Linda Vista house. She stored stuff in it. I had to crawl over old tools, bikes, and chairs to get to the spare room. Junk filled it, too.

"Clean this room out and you can use it," my Aunt Martha said.

I chose not to. It looked nothing like Hemingway's study in Cuba. Spiders lurked in every dusty corner. Maybe I should have taken the room. Maybe I could have launched my writing career from there. Maybe. But I doubt it.

Although my grandmother never said so, I think she wearied of this strange, monastic kid camping in her kitchen, pounding away on the typewriter.

"Why don't you clean out a room in your mother's house out back?" she asked.

My mother, too, had a Linda Vista house out back. My Uncle Peanut used to talk about sleeping in it. Then I found out he slept under it.

I went through the house. It brimmed with junk as well. I spent much of the day going through old boxes. I found papers from my great-grandfather in there. Notations in neat script. But I ran out of gas before I was done.

I never did get a nice place to write—a room of my own, with a desk and bookshelves and trophy game on the walls.

I joke that it was all that stood between me and fame.

Shopkeeper's Murder Still Raises Doubt

JUNE 10, 1999

A hundred years ago, on a day like today, Philip Stedman Sparkman would have been minding his general store at the foot of Palomar Mountain near the Rincon Indian Reservation in San Diego County.

Sparkman, an Englishman, took over the small country store at Rincon Springs around 1885, after a stint of keeping a store in Albuquerque, New Mexico.

Sparkman was a small man, slight of build, maybe 125 pounds with heavy shoes on. He had close-cropped red hair and a full red beard.

While in New Mexico, he learned Spanish, which came in handy in Rincon. Most of the two hundred or so Luiseño Indians who resided nearby didn't speak English, but did speak some Spanish, a holdover from the missionaries.

Because his was the only store within a ten-mile radius of the reservation, the Indians, plus a scattering of ranchers and homesteaders in the surrounding area, bought from him.

Set amid oak trees and sage, his store was a low adobe, described as dim and cool inside. Merchandise of all sorts—hardware, clothes, groceries—hung from pegs or was arranged on shelves.

Behind the counter, Sparkman, quiet and respectful, would wait on customers.

About thirty feet from the store, Sparkman built a small adobe home. He also added to the store a storeroom and a study.

Louis Salmons, who lived nearby in Pauma Valley, described Sparkman this way in a San Diego Historical Society interview:

> He was a very peculiar man. He ran the store there. You'd walk in the store, not only Indian but a stranger or anybody, and he'd stand there with his hand on the counter. He'd never ask you what you'd have, or anything of the kind. Just put his hand on the counter, and wait for you to pick out something....I'd go down to Sparkman's, and we'd sit and talk there till ten or eleven at night. He'd always have a bowl of little cakes and bring out a bottle of wine.

Blessed with a knack for languages, Sparkman thought it good for business to learn some Luiseño. What started as a fluke, however, became his life's passion. He thirsted to know more about his Indian neighbors.

He befriended many and interviewed them to learn their ways. He wrote down his findings.

Neighbors often saw his lamp glowing in the adobe house until way into the morning as he worked on his writings.

Eventually, Sparkman compiled a serviceable dictionary of the Luiseño language. He also wrote *The Culture of Luiseño Indians*, published in 1908 by the University of California.

He became an ethnographer.

For more than twenty years, Sparkman tended the store to make money, but studied Indian ways to make his mark in the world.

Shortly after nine p.m. on May 17, 1907, Philip Sparkman

sprawled face up in the Rincon dust, his back riddled with shotgun pellets, his red beard splattered with blood from his cut throat.

While Sparkman was reading a book on Indians in his adobe home, someone called out, asking him to open the store.

Sparkman set the book down. Thinking he would be right back, he left the kerosene lamp burning. Once inside the store, Sparkman took his customary place behind the counter.

The assailant raised a 12-gauge shotgun. Blam! A spray of pellets smacked Sparkman's shoulder. Sparkman ran for the back door, but it was locked. Another blast missed Sparkman but ripped through the door.

Sparkman ran out the front. He took no more than a few steps when a shot hit him square in the back, knocking him to the ground.

Then the man took a knife and slit Sparkman's throat. He went through Sparkman's pockets and stole a buckskin money pouch, but left $240 under the counter and $75 in gold in the metal box.

After an investigation, the San Diego County Sheriff arrested a Rincon Indian, a local ranch worker, for the Sparkman murder. Few people at the time thought the Indian did it. Nevertheless, he was arrested and held for trial. At a hearing on August 12, 1907, the jury declared him insane and sent him to the mental hospital in San Bernardino.

Doubts about his guilt remain.

Long Trip Gives a Glimpse into a Father's Eyes

JUNE 17, 1999

In the spring of 1960, we ordered summer clothes from the Sears catalog.

Traveling clothes. Lord have mercy, the Johnsons were going on vacation.

Before that, I'd never been on vacation. You see, for about two years, from when I was about two until I was four, I never saw my father. He was battling tuberculosis in a military hospital.

To a young boy, the red scar that slashed down my father's back was about the most exciting thing about him.

After doctors declared him fit, he emerged from the hospital and re-entered my life.

I had been living at my grandparents' house on the Pala Indian Reservation with my mother and sister.

I slept in my Uncle Copy's bedroom, where pictures of boxers and ballplayers covered the walls. I ate when hungry, played when the mood struck, combed my hair if I felt like it, and pestered my grandfather around the yard with never a rebuke.

I lived in freedom. That is, until my father arrived. In short order, he packed us up and moved us to Santa Clara, where he attended college and I learned to be civilized.

My father drilled us in table manners. It mattered to him which way the sheets unrolled from the toilet paper. He expected teeth to be brushed, hair to be combed, and faces to be scrubbed. I even ate dreaded creamed cod on toast. "People who don't eat are sick, and sick people go to bed," he said. It was creamed cod or the pillow.

To enforce his will, he carved a paddle from an oak plank and kept it handy above the refrigerator. With one move toward the paddle, he could reduce us kids to stuttering idiots.

Frankly, I resented my dad for stealing me from my easy reservation life. I loathed his rules and manners and morality. His starched, button-down world reeked of structure and discipline. I much preferred the sweet scent of fresh tortillas and lazy reservation days.

Though I made frequent returns to the reservation, they only made my Santa Clara life seem more dismal.

During his college years, my dad spent most of his time hitting the books. Oh, he popped in to make sure I downed my greens and chewed with my mouth closed, but I didn't see much of him.

Then he graduated and wanted to take us on vacation, a road trip through the western states.

Being enclosed in a car with mom, dad, and my three siblings— especially since my brother Paul was famous for getting carsick— wasn't my idea of a good time. But I had no choice.

My dad loaded up a yellow 1954 Plymouth station wagon powered by a flathead, six-cylinder engine. He hitched up a small teardrop trailer, the kind where the back end lifts up to reveal a kitchen. He lashed some trunks onto the roof-rack and we hit the blue highways to see America.

For about a month and half, we drove up California to the Pacific Northwest, up into British Columbia, down through Montana and states south.

We stopped in campgrounds for the night and ate lots of

hard-boiled eggs on the road. The smell of eggs on vinyl upholstery still unsettles me.

But the main thing was, I got to know my dad on that trip. I watched him. I saw his pale eyes reflected in the rearview mirror. I noted his smiles, his conversational tone, his interest in showing us the countryside.

In Nevada, we stayed for a couple of days in a campground near some mountains. The kids played while my dad fixed the trailer tire.

In Oregon and Washington, we visited his relatives and saw the house where he was born. It made him more human somehow.

In New Mexico, we camped by a river and my dad scrambled us eggs and kippered snacks.

When traveling through the desert, with the sun parching our throats, we stopped at a gas station. My dad made sure all of us had cold pop before he bought himself a drink. When it came to him, only a warm chocolate drink was left. Yet he didn't complain.

Before the trip, I had my doubts. But afterward, I knew my dad loved us.

Life Is Here. Life Is Now. Wait's Over.

Long ago, I figured real life for me wouldn't begin until some future time. Maybe then I'd have money to sip red wine in Paris bistros, walk barefoot on teak-decked sailing ships, or dance slow with sloe-eyed Pacific Island girls.

But I've since learned life is here, life is now. Can't put it on hold to wait for better. No, life waits for no one.

One summer morning, about thirty years ago, my grandmother opened the back-porch door to roust me.

"Time to get up, boy," she said.

I clambered out of my bunk, an iron-framed Army cot that sagged in the middle, to button on a pair of faded jeans, slip a T-shirt over my head, and lace on my work boots.

In the kitchen, my grandmother spooned beans, fried eggs, and bacon onto my plate, and nodded toward hot tortillas waiting in a covered bowl.

I sat down to eat, and my grandmother poured coffee into a brown mug for me. I hurried through breakfast. Any minute the Blue Hornet would honk out front.

And there it was, more a whimper than a honk, from a horn that shorted out.

I wrapped eggs, bacon, and beans into a breakfast burrito to go. As I ran out, my grandmother handed me a lunch bag.

Out front, the car smoked. I climbed into the back of a 1955 Ford, dubbed the Blue Hornet for its electric blue spray-paint job. Hank Howard, an old guy in bib overalls and a perpetual grin, sat up front, as did Hoolie Freeman, the man behind the wheel.

Seated in the back were Verle "Chicken" Rodriguez and Victor Smith, two guys from Pala. Next we had to pick up my cousin Juggie Magee at his adobe house down the road on the Pala Indian Reservation.

Hoolie ground the car into first, and gunned the six-cylinder engine. The clutch slipped, but we jerked into motion nonetheless.

At Juggie's we squealed to a stop. Again Hoolie honked. But no answer. As usual, Juggle was late. I ran into his house to find him looking for his other boot.

"Come on, let's go," I said.

Juggie jeered at me with his glass eye, as if to say, "I go when I'm ready."

Finally he found the boot behind the couch and limped with one boot out to the car.

First we had to take Hank Howard, who may have been seventy at the time, to his irrigation job at an orange grove up Highway 76.

Hank had a fifth of wine in his lunch box, which he dared not pull out, or the boys might drain it before he got to work. He intended it to last at least until lunch.

We drove the backcountry roads, Hoolie working the gears like a big-rig driver with too much load.

The Blue Hornet's shabby interior reeked of port wine, stale tobacco, and old man smell.

"Can't we crack open a window?" I asked.

I fumbled to light a Camel to cover the smell.

We dropped Hank off, and continued on to the Miramar Naval Air Station, where the four of us worked at the horse stables.

Once past Escondido, we had to take the freeway. If the car, which had a bad front end, exceeded fifty-five miles per hour, it would shimmy faster than Elvis Presley's hips. Hoolie kept it slow out of fear the car might shake itself apart.

From the freeway, we bounced into the stable's dirt parking area, dust rooster-tailing behind us.

Once stopped, Hoolie threw open his door and stepped out. Chicken, his gray hair pomaded back, looked pale. Noting he had been wordless the whole ride down, I guessed he nursed a wicked hangover. He went straight to a faucet and splashed cold water on his face.

Before getting to work, we checked in at the front office, where a young secretary marked our time cards.

The Miramar stables had both sway-backed horses for rent and fancier horses boarded by officers' daughters for shows and such.

Most of the rental stock roamed loose in a big corral. Every morning we had to cut out a dozen or so for riding that day. We roped some of the more ornery horses. Hoolie, an old cowboy, was best with the rope.

With the horses tethered to hitching posts, we saddled them up.

Next we mucked stalls, raking out the ammonia-soaked droppings.

Chicken, oh-so-hungover, would ease himself into a pipe stall and gag at the ripeness.

"Hello, horsie," he'd say, in a low voice.

And that would be our morning—rake the droppings into a pile, scoop them into a wheelbarrow, and dump them into a big compost heap.

Victor, a big southpaw, sometimes stood like a boxer in front of a horse. "My right will cut you, but my left will knock you out," he'd tell an obstinate horse.

It might move, or it might step on Vic's foot.

We ate lunch, sitting on our haunches in the shade of the barn. Chicken brought yellow chilies fresh from his garden. He passed them around and my teeth crunched into the sweet heat. I gulped Mountain Dew from a vending machine and munched my grandmother's bean and hamburger tortilla rolls.

After lunch we cleaned stalls in the big barn. Young girls, fourteen or fifteen years old, spent the afternoon brushing their horses and braiding their manes into uniform rows.

On the day in question, a guy we knew, Pete, pulled up in his pickup after lunch. His son, Tommy, from the Barona Indian Reservation, was a lead hand at the stable. Pete popped open his glove compartment and pulled out a pint of Black Velvet. He held it out. I joined the others in taking a shot. I grimaced as the sun-hot whiskey sloshed down my throat.

After that, some horses kicked up a ruckus in the corral, so we checked on the commotion. The stables had a stud Shetland pony who thought he was king of the hill.

He was trying to mount a mare and she was having none of it. She fended him off, but he was not easily dissuaded. Scotty, the stable boss, told us to get him out of there before either he or the mare got hurt.

Juggie, bolstered by the Black Velvet, led the way. We did our best to get the pony out quietly, but the little booger bucked and kicked and bit. Hoolie had to get a rope around his neck, and we dragged him to a pipe stall. I've never seen a madder pony.

A girl, about my age, drove up in her father's Mercedes-Benz. She wore Levi cutoffs and a blue work shirt tied above the waist. She was dark-skinned with a sprinkling of freckles across her nose. Her long, black hair glinted in the sun and my heart cartwheeled.

She strode toward the barn to ready her Appaloosa for an afternoon ride. I flashed her a winning smile, but to her, I would forever be a stable boy. She stepped on my heart the way she might accidentally step in manure.

At quitting time, Scotty opened a case of Coors and we swallowed cold beer. On his second beer, Chicken cracked a smile.

On my second beer, I felt better too. Even the girl didn't bother me anymore—much.

Long ago, I thought life hadn't really begun for me. But thirty years later, I know now I was wrong. Life is here, life is now.

Scouring the Trails with a Teen's Best Pal

October 28, 1999

Back in my teens I had a German shorthair pointer named Brine.

Big and rangy, he loved nothing better than to roam the backcountry with me.

He'd scamper after a cottontail or a covey of quail and disappear into the brush. Sometimes he'd wander off so long I'd worry. But I'd whistle and soon see his liver spots emerge from a tangle of manzanita and buckwheat, a smile on his chops, his stumpy tail wagging.

One morning we took off up the canyon, west of the reservation by the old windmill. We called it a windmill, but it was just a rusting tower topped with metal blades that once pumped water for livestock there. In later years, young people parked there to drink beer around a night fire.

About daybreak, Brine and I walked the sandy trails of the lower canyon and then broke trail to ascend the mountains. We climbed several hours, fighting through dry thickets of brush, with branches and stickers scratching my arms and poking through my jeans.

Way back up there, in a small saddle in the middle of nowhere, I happened upon an abandoned shack.

Brush had overtaken most of the yard, but the wooden walls of the shack still stood.

Curiously, no road led to the place, and I wondered who had built it and why. I poked around a few minutes but saw nothing but a few rusty cans, so we headed back.

Brine and I stuck to deer trails when we could, but mostly we cut through the rough stuff. Back at the canyon head, we stopped for a rest under some trees.

While sitting on a rock I spotted some bone half-covered by dirt and grass. I walked over and found more bone, picked clean and bleached by the sun.

Bones lay everywhere. Leg bones, rib bones, hip bones all over the landscape. I picked up a jawbone and saw sharp teeth like a dog's.

My heart raced. Had I stumbled onto a coyote graveyard?

I seemed to remember that once, while looking through a *National Geographic* for bare-breasted women, I had seen something about elephant graveyards, where tusks and bone littered the ground. Did coyotes, feeling death approach, drag themselves to this spot to die?

Even Brine seemed excited, sniffing about, pawing the earth. I walked home thinking I should alert *National Geographic* to my discovery.

At home, my grandfather sat at an outside table listening to talk radio.

"Gramps," I said hurriedly, "I found a coyote graveyard."

"A what?" he asked.

I described the bones scattered far back into the canyon.

He didn't actually say I was full of beans, but a glint in his eye betrayed his disbelief.

Several days later, I bragged to my old buddy Jean Jackson about the bones and explained in detail my coyote graveyard theory, how by instinct they crawled to this mystical ground to die with their kind.

At least he waited for me to finish before he busted out laughing.

"Well, young man, if you wanna know something, that's where I dump the carcasses of the coyotes and bobcats I trap," he said. "I take them over there so they can rot in peace, without the smell bothering anybody."

I knew Jean trapped every winter, but I never asked him what he did with the remains. My high ideas thudded to the ground, and I knew I would be in for some future ribbing.

Cautiously, I asked him about the old shack I had found.

Turns out, there was a woman on the reservation nicknamed B-19. She was married to a Navy guy who had a Navy buddy who built the shack.

One of his arms was missing, presumably lost in battle, and he built that shack up that roadless mountainside to get away from the world. Somehow, he packed in building supplies. And no joke, it had to be a struggle.

As the story goes, he lived up there, fashioning furniture from branches, twining them like wicker to make chairs and such. But he hasn't been heard from since the 1950s.

Brine is long gone, too.

Remembering the Low Tide of Puppy Love

APRIL 13, 2000

Oceanside's waves unfurled flat and disheveled, not much good for surfing, so Bear and I decided to walk the beach instead of wasting about on lazy swells.

Unhurried, we made footprints along the wet sand of low tide, watching sandpipers race-walk after sand crabs, seagulls wheel and trill after a kid throwing Fritos, and winter-white beachcombers redden with their first sun.

A man in black swim trunks and a sleeveless shirt flew a kite that looked exactly like a mallard drake. Even a passing seagull was duped into belligerence.

A pale moon rose on the beach as a heavy-thighed woman in a thong swimsuit clambered up from her beach towel.

A four-pack of nymphets in shimmering swimsuits strolled the strand like it was a fashion runway. They preened and giggled and paraded.

"So Dad, what was the beach like in the sixties?" Bear asked.

Bear likes to quiz me about the 1960s. And now that he's learning to surf, he wants to hear old surfing stories too. Unfortunately, I didn't surf in the sixties. But I tell him what I can.

In the 1960s, I remember Santa Cruz and Oceanside. I told him of the longboards, the noseriding, the early wetsuits, the beach jalopies I saw.

We walked in easy conversation, the sun to our right, and I thought it a good time to broach a touchy subject. I had overheard hints that things had gone south between him and a girl he liked. Maybe it would help if I shared my own eighth-grade puppy-love experiences.

So I let Bear into my personal past: in the sixties, just as they do today, beach goddesses romped in the foam in two-piece bathing suits. Most beach bunnies lived to tan. They rubbed in Coppertone or baby oil and fried in the sun. They daubed on white lipstick and avoided wetting their pouffy hairdos.

But the object of my affections, Betty, was an archetypal surfer girl who didn't fear wet hair. She had long, straight, sun-bleached locks. She wasn't tall and lanky, but shorter, with a swimmer's musculature, about 5 foot 2, eyes of blue, and freckles peppering her nose.

She loved the sea. She had an older brother who surfed, so she surfed, too. Her parents owned a Santa Cruz summer beach house, and she turned coconut brown at the first sign of spring.

She had a way of standing with both hands on one hip in an orange bikini that sent me into a tailspin.

While other girls wore saddle shoes or penny loafers with their Catholic-school plaid skirts, she wore blue deck shoes—Keds.

She was the little surfer girl the Beach Boys sang about.

For a week or two, toward the end of eighth grade, mutual friends coupled up, and we were thrown together by default. It was either sit with me or sit alone. She sat with me. After talking to her, I found we shared birthdays—a sure sign, in my mind, the heavens intended eternal love.

Lovesick, I lost weight. I stammered in her presence. Clammy jitters possessed me when I shared a chocolate soda with her.

In those days, surf boys wore baby-blue Levis, blue Keds, and bleeding Madras shirts, the kind imported from India with colors that ran when washed in hot water.

Nothing else would do. "Please, Mom, please buy me a Madras shirt!" I begged. Mom bought me some wannabe Gemco shirt. It wouldn't bleed if I stabbed it with a knife. How could I wear it to the big end-of-school party? I wore a Hang-Ten T-shirt instead.

Tiki torches burned in the backyard of the big party. Betty and I danced close and sweaty to the Beach Boys and Motown. We ate steak teriyaki on a skewer with pineapple. We snuck into a darkened room for a make-out session. My, my, my. I felt skewered by her kisses.

Afterward, I dreamed of how great our lives would be together. Ours would be an endless summer.

A couple of days later, with no hint of troubles, Betty dumped me for a friend of mine. I guess he was cooler than me. After all, he had a silver tooth.

"And so you see, son, Betty broke my heart," I said.

He smiled. And I ached a little.

Boxing Fan Hit with Changes at the Fights

APRIL 20, 2000

Back in the days when we turned the TV channels with pliers, my grandfather and I regularly watched boxing.

We'd sit on the couch, chile verde burritos in hand, and peer through the snow at black-and-white telecasts of fights from the Olympic in Los Angeles. He'd drink tall cans of Lucky Lager and I'd have Pepsi, and we'd cheer favorite fighters and give the Bronx cheer to tomato cans.

And even before we had TV, we'd listen to static-filled radio broadcasts of greats like Rocky Marciano, Sugar Ray Robinson, and Archie Moore.

Later, when I was a young reporter for The Associated Press, I'd occasionally cover fights from the Olympic, and I'd send printouts of my stories to my grandfather. As I improved as a reporter, I wrote A-wire stories about politics, about serial killers, about major disasters, but nothing pleased my grandfather like the short pieces I wrote about boxing.

I'll always remember those boxing moments with my grandfather. All these years later, I'm still a fan.

So for some Saturday night fun, I went to Fight Night at the Pechanga Entertainment Center.

Boxing has changed much since the beer-and-peanut days at the Olympic. For one thing, twenty-five years ago you'd be hard-pressed to find a woman in attendance. In the old days, boxing was boys' night out, a chance for beer-bellied men to hoop and holler and stink if they wanted to.

But these days, women enjoy the fights. Pechanga Fight Nights are like date nights—older married couples, younger sweethearts—and some women come in man-less groups just to be part of the action.

Used to be you could show up to fights in torn jeans and a stretched-out T-shirt and nobody cared. But more and more men arrive in sports coats with stylish women in high heels on their arms.

I don't remember women boxers at the Olympic. But Pechanga often schedules at least one female bout. These days, women box.

Saturday night, Daisy Ocasio squared off with Britt Van Buskirk. Early in the fight, you could tell Van Buskirk was better. It wasn't long before she drilled Ocasio with a crushing right that folded Ocasio to the canvas.

No messing around. These women can punch.

I don't remember ring-card girls in the old days either, but from my perspective anyway, they've added a welcome dimension to contemporary fights. Ring-card girls in the skimpiest of attire parade around the ring to help onlookers keep the round count.

Beer-bellied men whistle their appreciation as the women pass by. I'm not sure what women think about it all. Judging from some frowns, it might be, "Humph, what has she got that I haven't got?"

To add to the charged atmosphere, Pechanga recently added beer sales to Fight Night, so men could keep beer bellies at full girth.

I'm not much in favor of the beer sales. It's not that I'm some holier-than-thou teetotaler disgusted by those who indulge. Heck, as far as I'm concerned, if you have a designated driver, knock yourself out.

It's just that beer can really bring out the obnoxious in people, myself included. Saturday night, I sat near this beer-bellied guy in his late fifties wearing a loud T-shirt and a car-racing cap who wouldn't shut the heck up.

In the beginning, before the beer started flowing, he was a mild-mannered chap. But the waitress kept 'em coming, and his motor got oiled up. I mean well-oiled.

Nonstop with the motormouth, he goaded the fighters: "Remember what I taught you...okay, right, left, and uppercut... come on, you bum, do like I told you." His face got redder, his voice got louder, and I wanted to buy him a couple of beers in hopes he'd pass out.

No matter, I saw some good fights. I saw a kid from Fontana, Lafayette Randolph, dance and counterpunch his way to his second win.

I saw former three-time world champion Wilfredo Vazquez take it to a gutsy but outclassed Russell Mosley from San Diego.

I saw some good action. I just wish my grandfather, a Pechanga member, could have lived to see it too.

He'd Rather be Tapping out of Dance Shows

June 29, 2000

I'm not a dance person. Never have been. I blame my traumatized youth.

You see, my little sister, like most girls of the 1950s, took tap. She had a dance-class album she played remorselessly, over and over, purposely trying to ruin any future enjoyment of dance for me.

To this day I'm haunted by the recorded horror of a Wally Cox–like voice, nasal and monotonous, calling out "step, shuffle, ball-change," punctuated by the spasmodic clacking of taps against the floor. Her dance steps sounded like a herd of sharp-hoofed warthogs scrambling for footing on waxed linoleum.

If that wasn't bad enough, there was the occasional family recital. Sometimes, after dinner, my sister donned her leotard, stepped into her patent leather shoes, and tapped out her routine while my brother accompanied her on his accordion. Oh, Lordy! She stepped, shuffled, and ball-changed to my brother's barely decipherable version of "Camptown Races." I didn't know whether to laugh or spew. No wonder I'm scarred.

I grew up, grew long hair, grew a beard. I smoked Camels,

guzzled beer with tattooed buddies, listened to rock 'n' roll, and feigned coolness. I did what I could to conceal my ugly past. How could I ever live down the truth of my origins?

As I aged, I breathed easier. I figured dance was behind me, an ordeal I'd never have to confront again.

Then I had a daughter. My wife thought she owed it to her gender to enroll my daughter in dance. I dutifully paid for lessons and attended recitals to witness my daughter in a yellow leotard with glued-on tail feathers do the chicken dance.

More step, shuffle, ball-change. More bad music. More horror.

Thankfully, my daughter's dance teacher saw the light and quit, mercifully ending my daughter's dance career. My second daughter had sense enough to dislike tap. Once again, the years distanced me from dance. Gone for good, I thought.

Yet, Saturday, I sat in a recital hall, waiting for my granddaughter, Sukmal, three, to perform the duck dance. I checked the program and found I'd have to endure twenty such dances before my granddaughter's performance.

Girls tapped. Girls spun. Girls cartwheeled. But when it came time for my granddaughter to shake her tail feathers, I heard an emphatic "No" echo from backstage. I recognized the voice. I knew my granddaughter had refused to go on.

Sure enough, a raft of dancing ducks shuffled across the stage sans Sukie.

The next day, recovered from her dancing upheaval, Sukie and I sat in the balcony of the Riverside Municipal Auditorium for the Redlands Festival Ballet Company's performance of *Cinderella*.

I wanted Sukie to see real dancers. To sense what could be done with effort. I wanted her to experience dance.

Sukie wore an ankle-length flowery dress with a cloth hat. Lavender polish glistened from her nails. Fake miniature pearls decorated her neck and wrist. She appeared quite the ballet connoisseur.

The lights dimmed, the red velvet curtain ascended, and dancers leaped and twirled and pranced on tiptoe. Sukie seemed to like it. She clapped with enthusiasm.

Me, I wondered if a hot blues band might be playing at Lake Alice's up the road. I fidgeted. I studied the wrought-iron chandeliers.

Don't get me wrong. I have a lot of admiration for dancers. They are as fit and hardworking as any trained athlete.

Once, about four years ago, my editor assigned me to do a story on an eleven-year-old girl who showed great promise as a dancer. I groaned at the prospect, but after seeing her work, I had great respect for her.

In fact, she was in this production. Now an accomplished sixteen-year-old, Julia Olsen-Rodriguez shined on stage.

But dance in general...Well, my sister ruined dance for me.

So, when Sukie said she wanted to go home after the first act, I didn't argue. On the way home, Sukie fell asleep in her car seat, probably dreaming of fairy godmothers.

I looked at her, thinking, "The things you do for love."

Closing a Portal to Past; Opening One to Promise

AUGUST 17, 2000

Metal against metal, like a blacksmith hammering a horseshoe, a pile driver clangs on the Pala Indian Reservation.

From morning till night, weighted machinery bangs pylons into the sand of the San Luis Rey River bottom.

The clanging has become the metronome of our lives, measuring the moments until we become "Casino Indians."

Work has begun on the gaming facility that many dream will lift us to a new prosperity.

Day by day, the casino takes shape on what used to be Acorn Park, the old campgrounds. At least a dozen old oak trees were yanked out to make way for the casino. A snarl of sawed limbs tangled on a bare spot of earth is all that remains. Work crews will cut trees into cordwood and distribute it to elders.

We drove by the other day, and my son noticed all the construction. "It's all going to change, Dad," Bear said. "It's never going to be the same, is it?"

"Not likely," I replied.

Bear turned wistful about the campground, about the fiesta

nights there, sitting around fires and watching peon games until early morning.

He thinks of the casino as an interloper, an interruption to a lifestyle he's grown up in. But then, Bear has never known real poverty the way some Pala Indians have known poverty. Which is why I've tried to remain neutral about the casino.

People often ask me about Indian casinos.

As I've written before, I'm not a fan of casinos. I rarely go into them, except to watch boxing or hear some music, or to graze on cheap steak and eggs. I don't gamble much. In a casino, I play a little slow death (keno), drink a few free cocktails, and people-watch.

Oh, I'll sit down to a little poker with the boys, and I don't mind a two-dollar bet here and there on the horses. But I simply hate to lose. The pain of losing exceeds the joy of winning.

Bottom line, I wish Indians could find a more dignified way of achieving prosperity. I hate to think of the addicted gamblers who gamble away their happiness, ruin their families, lose not only their lives but their sense of self-worth. So I challenge Indian casinos to spot problem gamblers and offer help in the way of counseling.

Yes, gaming has downsides, but for now, Indians view gaming as a portal to the American dream. And I think it's time Indians got a seat at the banquet table. So I back the Indian's right to sovereignty and self-determination and the choice to pursue gaming as a livelihood.

Pala Indians have been poor for a long time, but they've also been able to turn hardship into a laughing matter.

For instance, an Indian couple stops at the grocery store.

"What are we stopping here for?" the man asks.

"I need to pick up some Indian steak," the woman replies.

The man nods his head, leans back, and listens to the game on the radio.

The woman heads not for the meats, but for the deli counter.

Oscar Mayer? No, the house brand is cheaper. She grabs a couple of packs of bologna.

On the rez, "Indian steak" means bologna. Unable to afford T-bone or porterhouse, we bought bologna. We ate it for breakfast. Ever have fried bologna and powdered eggs? For lunch, on tortillas with mayo and mustard. For dinner, in thick sandwiches on Wonder Bread with commodity cheese.

In the not-too-bygone days, an Indian car was something to behold. Used to be, you could even go into an Indian shop and buy an "Indian Car" bumper sticker.

An Indian car was most properly a long, low, dented-up gas hog with a straightened clothes hanger for a radio antenna. No self-respecting Indian car had all of its hubcaps. Seat covers might be an olive-drab Army blanket to keep seat springs from poking you in the rear. Hang a couple of feathers from the rearview mirror and pour in some Ray Lube oil so it didn't smoke too much, and you had a prize Indian car fit for the powwow highway.

Maybe, once the casino arrives, we can drive all the Indian cars to the junkyard where they belong.

Fire Up the Pit to Barbecue the Bird

November 23, 2000

This Thanksgiving, like last Thanksgiving, I will pit-barbecue a turkey. In addition to the turkey, I may throw in a pot roast or a leg of lamb or something else I like, since turkey, at least in my book, is more traditional than tasty. Turkey is the Wally Cox of poultry, bland by nature and often as dry as a lecture on socioeconomics.

But the family expects turkey on Thanksgiving, so I'll oblige them. Pit barbecuing rescues the gobbler from monotony, allowing it to steam in smoky juices. It even tastes good to me.

About forty years ago, my buddy Jean Jackson installed a permanent roasting pit in his yard. He shoveled out a hole deep enough to accommodate a fifty-gallon drum, then poured concrete around it.

The drum eventually burned out, leaving a concrete-lined excavation, perfect for the pit barbecue.

Briefly, the pit barbecue works like this:

First, take a good amount of wood, a hardwood like oak or hickory or even seasoned eucalyptus in a pinch, and let it burn down so there's a layer at least six inches deep of glowing coals at the pit's bottom. The more meat you cook, the more coals you need.

On top of the wood, you can place football-size rocks (lava rocks work best) and they'll heat up in the fire as well. The rocks, however, are not critical. The meat will cook fine without them. It's your choice.

While the fire is doing its work, season the meat with salt, pepper, and garlic, onion, and chili powder, or if you prefer, a commercial barbecue rub or one of your own concoctions. A favorite marinade also works.

Once the meat is seasoned, wrap it in aluminum foil. A double layer is a good idea to keep the juices in.

Some barbecuers also recommend encasing the meat in muslin at this juncture. Old sheets or pillowcases will suffice. For the most part, I eliminate the muslin step. I've done it both with muslin and without, and I can't see the muslin difference.

Next, place the foil-wrapped meat into wet burlap sacks. You want the burlap to be damp, but not so soaked that water douses your coals.

Finally, take baling wire or unraveled clothes hangers and wrap the whole burlap package the way you might wrap a birthday present. Make a handle of wire at this point. It makes it easier to retrieve the bundles from the pit.

When the coals have burned down to a flameless, glowing red, put the meat in. Just gentle the bundles onto the coals. Don't worry, they won't burn.

Put a lid over the pit. Jean has a disk of steel like a manhole cover for his pit. Other people use lengths of roofing tin.

Now, here's the most important step. You must cover the lid with sand so the heat stays in and no air leaks out. You want an airtight oven, where heat and steam will slow-cook the meat. A layer of sand over the entire pit about four or five inches thick usually does the trick.

Once you've covered the pit, look carefully for telltale signs of smoke or steam leaking through the sand. Sometimes spraying the top with a little water from a hose will help identify any leaks.

If you see little plumes of smoke working through, just shovel more sand to cover them.

I usually leave the meat in overnight. Say, if I have a turkey and a roast cooking, I'll put them in at midnight and pull them out at noon. You should allow at least eight hours of cooking time, and more time won't hurt. Over time, the coals lose their intense heat and the pit becomes a big warming oven, so you usually can leave the meat in there until you're ready to eat without its drying out or burning.

This whole process goes a lot smoother if you have a beer or two. At least for me, beer makes it more fun, less an ordeal.

When it's time, shovel off the sand and lift off the cover. It's always a bit of a surprise when it comes out. It's no sure thing. But I've never had a turkey disaster. In fact, it's the best turkey I've ever eaten, smoky and spicy and moist.

One more important ingredient. Cook it with love. The best spice of all.

About the Author

Gordon Johnson is a Cahuilla/Cupeño from the Pala Indian Reservation in San Diego County, California. A former columnist and feature writer for the *Riverside Press-Enterprise*, he is the author of a book of collected columns, *Rez Dogs Eat Beans*, that was translated and published in the Czech Republic. He is also a contributor to the recent anthology of Inland Empire writers published by Heyday Books, *Inlandia*. Johnson lives in Pala and is working on his master of fine arts degree at Antioch University, Los Angeles.

HEYDAY INSTITUTE

Since its founding in 1974, Heyday Books has occupied a unique niche in the publishing world, specializing in books that foster an understanding of the history, literature, art, environment, social issues, and culture of California and the West. We are a 501(c)(3) nonprofit organization based in Berkeley, California, serving a wide range of people and audiences.

We thank the following for their help in launching and supporting Heyday's California Indian Publishing Program:

Anthony Andreas, Jr.; Barona Band of Mission Indians; Fred & Jean Berensmeier; Black Oak Casino; Buena Vista Rancheria; Candelaria Fund; Columbia Foundation; Colusa Indian Community Council; Lawrence E. Crooks; Judith & Brad Croul, in memory of Harry Fonseca; Patricia A. Dixon; Elk Valley Rancheria; Marion E. Greene; Hopland Band of Pomo Indians; LEF Foundation; Morongo Band of Mission Indians; National Endowment for the Arts; San Francisco Foundation; Sandy Cold Shapero; Ernest & June Siva, in honor of the Dorothy Ramon Learning Center; Thendara Foundation; Tomioka Family, in memory of Taeko Tomioka; Tom White; Harold and Alma White Memorial Fund

For more information about Heyday Institute, our publications and programs, please visit our website at www.heydaybooks.com.